Contents

A POCKET GUIDE TO
Hawaiian Lei Making

A Step-by-Step Guide to Making Flower, Crochet, Straw, Rickrack, Money, and Shell Lei

Judy Dela Cruz
and Laurie Ide

Mutual Publishing

ISBN: 978-1-949307-73-3
Library of Congress Catalog Card Number available upon request

Design by Jane Gillespie
First Printing, March 2025

Mutual Publishing, LLC
1215 Center Street, Suite 210
Honolulu, Hawai'i 96816
Ph: (808) 732-1709
Fax: (808) 734-4094
email: info@mutualpublishing.com
www.mutualpublishing.com

Printed in South Korea

Flower Lei

The Hawaiian Lei

Throughout the history of ancient Hawai'i, men and women wore bone, shell, feather, hair, and stone garlands to beautify themselves and to distinguish themselves from others. They also used decorative foliage, seeds, fruit, and colorful flowers—now known in Hawai'i as a lei.

In modern times, the lei has become a symbol of Hawai'i—one that expresses aloha or love, friendship, and affection.

The art of lei making in Hawai'i has changed with each new innovative idea. A lei may also be made with man-made materials such as paper, ribbon, fabric, candy, currency, and even golf balls.

Lei Customs

Today, the lei is traditionally presented around the head and on the shoulders of a special someone. This custom began with the Hawaiian cultural value that the head and shoulders are sacred parts of the body. The lei is worn gracefully over the shoulders, draped both in the front as well as in the back. However, there are no rules written in today's modern society.

Almost any type of lei may be given to anyone as a token or gift of friendship. Presenting someone with a lei represents the admiration, respect, and honor given toward the individual. The lei is also given for special occasions and celebrations such as birthdays, graduations, anniversaries, weddings, and all special moments in one's life. The lei may even be made or bought for oneself to wear. The placement of the lei is traditionally followed by a kiss which represents love, a wish of luck, or aloha.

During the Boat Days of the late 1800s and early 1900s, visitors who arrived or departed on the steamships from the Hawaiian Islands received a lei as a gift of aloha. It is said that many departing visitors would throw their lei into the sea as the ship passed Diamond Head hoping the lei would float back to the beaches of the island. This would signify that he or she would also return to the islands some day.

Today, the giving of a lei to someone who is departing or arriving to the islands continues, but the lei is often kept as a memento of its beauty, fragrance, and for those special memories of aloha.

Lei Making Methods

There are six lei making methods: 1) Kui—stringing pattern; kui pololei is a straight, single pattern; kui poepoe is a circular, double pattern; kui lau is a back-and-forth pattern. 2) Hili or hilo—braiding, weaving pattern. 3) Wili—twining, twisting pattern. 4) Humu humu papa or humupapa—sewing with a needle and thread. 5) Haku—setting or mounting against a background material. 6) Kipuu, hipuu, nipuu—tying together, knotted pattern. The flower lei in this chapter are made using the first two methods: kui—stringing flowers together on a piece of thread and hili—braiding or weaving.

Lei Making Needles

A modern addition to the art of lei making, metal needles, have greatly expanded what types of lei can be made. The ancient Hawaiians had no metals, thus no needles.

A long, stainless steel needle (often made in Hawai'i) can be found at a florist or craft store.

This special needle is sharpened to a point at one end, while the other end is bent to a flat "eye" to hook on the thread. After threading, this eye must be flat so that blossoms can slide over it smoothly, preventing breakage.

The needles used in lei making vary in length and thickness. They range from 3-14" long and are available in thin, medium, and thick grades.

The most common stainless steel needle used for stringing lei is the 12" long, medium grade needle.

Cigar Lei

The cigar lei is made using the blossoms of a crape myrtle shrub which has 3/4" long tubular, slender, orange-red blossoms with black 6-tipped teeth and a white speck mouth resembling a miniature lit cigar tipped with white ash; no fragrance.

Lei Characteristics: Very long-lasting; popular to ship to the mainland. Lei will last up to fourteen days if refrigerated when not in use.

Season/Harvest Period: Year-round; blooms in intervals throughout the year; low in the hot summer months July through August. Pick blossoms in the early morning or evening when cool. The flowers are soft during the midday.

Storage: Sprinkle lightly with water. Place in plastic bag or container. Refrigerate. May be revived by soaking in cold water in the refrigerator for 4 hours. Shake off excess water.

Materials

- Medium 12" lei needle
- 104" length 3-ply twine or #10 crochet thread, folded in half. Tie a double knot about 6 inches from the open end of the string. Hook on the lei needle.

Quantity

- 70 blossoms for a 40" single lei, kui pololei, straight pattern
- 1,800 blossoms for a 40" double lei, kui poepoe, circular pattern

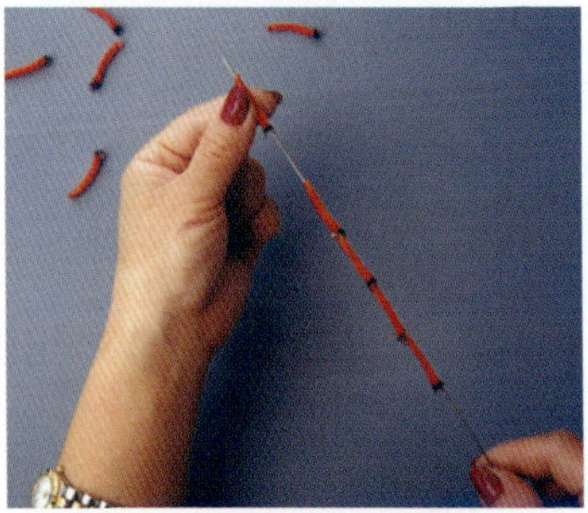

1. Pierce about 5 blossoms, starting at the top of the blossom. Gently hold blossoms and pulled own to the knotted end of the string. Continue until lei is 40" long (see Figure A on p. 5).

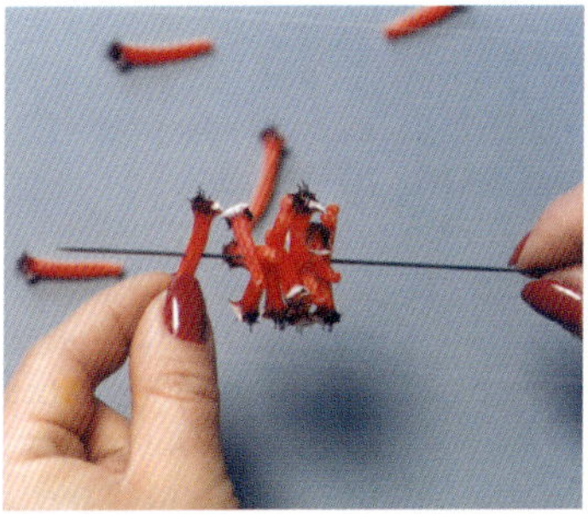

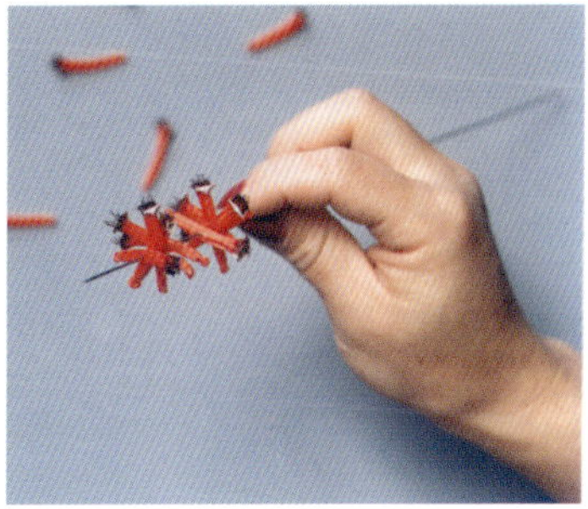

2. Pierce about 150 blossoms, placing 9 to 10 blossoms in a circular pattern. Pierce laterally through the center of the blossom, keeping the outside ends even. Place the second row of blossoms between the blossoms of the first row. Gently hold blossoms and pull down to the knotted end of the string. Continue until lei is 40" long (see Figure B).

3. Pierce 5 blossoms in a half-circular pattern for a double patterned lei. Place a second layer of 5 blossoms between the first layer blossoms. Continue until about 5" is pierced. Gently hold blossoms and pull down to knotted end of string. Continue until 40" long. A spiral pattern should form naturally (see Figure C).

Cigar Lei Patterns

A. Kui pololei, single lei, straight pattern
B. Kui poepoe, double lei, circular pattern
C. Kui poepoe, double patterned lei, circular pattern

Crown Flower Lei

The crown flower lei is made with the pale lavender or white blossoms of a milkweed shrub. The milk sap, in large doses, is extremely toxic. Remove sap from skin to prevent irritation. Use hand lotion before picking and stringing so sap does not stick to your skin.

Lei Characteristics: Versatile lei styles; lasts two to three days.

Season/Harvest Period: Year-round, peaking in the summer. Pick the blossoms in the early or mid-morning when cool.

Storage: Keep dry and airtight. Store in a damp newspaper. Place in a plastic bag or container and refrigerate.

Materials

- Medium 12" lei needle
- 52" 3-ply lei twine for figures 1, 3, 9, and 10.
- Figure 4 requires 208" twine folded in fourths.
- Figure 5 requires 106" twine folded in half plus 56-57 pieces for the rings. Tie a double knot about 6" from one end of the string. Hook on the lei needle.

Quantity

- 60-65 blossoms for a 40" single with petal lei, kui pololei, straight pattern
- 70-75 blossoms for a 40" single without petal lei, kui pololei straight pattern
- 350-400 blossoms for a large petal lei, kui pololei, straight pattern
- 450-480 blossoms for a 40" ring lei, kui pololei, fancy pattern
- 225 lavender blossoms and 225 white blossoms for a 40 ring and blossom lei, kui pololei, straight, fancy pattern
- 160 blossoms for a 40" double, ½ crown, rickrack lei, kui poepoe, circular pattern
- 184 blossoms for a 40" double ⅕ crown, rick-rack lei, kui poepoe, circular pattern

1. Pinch off the stems for a single lei with petals. Pierce about 6 blossoms. Gently hold the blossoms and pull down to the knotted end of the string. Continue until the lei is 40" long (see Figure A on p. 9).

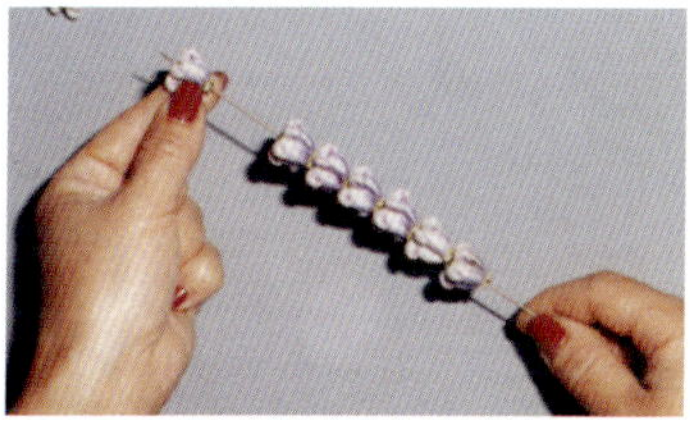

3. Pierce about 7 crowns. Gently hold crowns and pull down to knotted end of the string. Continue until 40" long (see Figure B on p. 9).

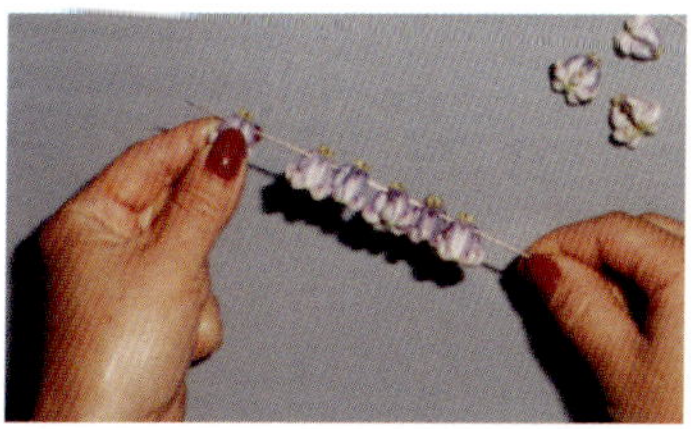

5. String 60 sets of 7 lavender crowns onto a 7" thread by piercing the sides of the blossoms. Tie a square knot, creating rings (see ring lei, Figure D on p. 9).

2. Break off the crown tops from the blossoms for a single lei without petals.

4. Pierce about 20 blossoms for a straight petal lei. Gently grasp blossoms and pull down to the knotted end of the string. Continue until 40" long (see Figure C on p. 9).

6. String 30 sets of 7 white crowns onto a 7" thread by piercing the sides of the blossoms. String 30 sets of 7 lavender crowns for a ring blossom lei. Tie each 7" strand of thread with a square knot, creating rings (see Figure E on p. 9)

7. Pierce a white crown starting at the base end. Add a white ring, face down, followed by a lavender crown blossom then a lavender ring, face down. Repeat the pattern for Figure E. For Figure D, pull off petal of blossoms.

8. Repeat until about 6 sets are pierced. Gently hold blossoms and pull down to the knotted end of the string. Continue until 40" long.

9. Break the crowns into halves. Discard the extra ¹/₅ segment. Pierce about 20 segments placing 3 in a circular pattern. Gently hold the blossoms and pull down to the knotted end of the string. Continue until lei is 40" long (see Figure F).

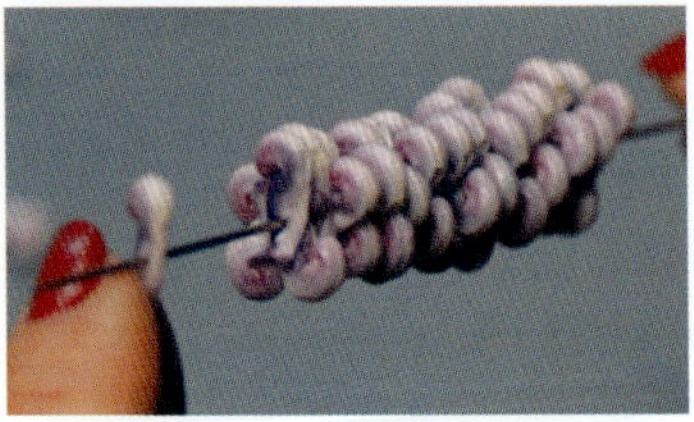

10. Break crowns into ¹/₅ segments. Pierce about 30 segments, placing 5 in a circular pattern. Gently hold the blossoms and pull down to the knotted end of the string. Continue until the lei is 40" long (see Figure G).

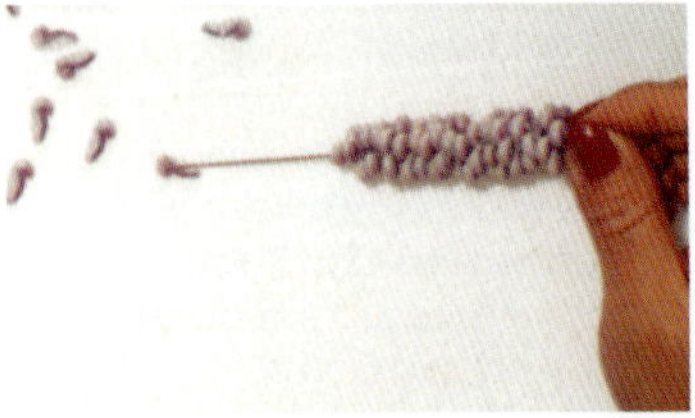

11. A Styrofoam base may be used to pierce the blossom segments.

Crown Flower Lei Patterns

A. Kui pololei, single with petal lei, straight pattern

B. Kui pololei, single without petal lei, straight pattern

C. Kui pololei, petal lei, straight pattern

D. Kui pololei, ring lei, fancy pattern

E. Kui pololei, ring and blossom lei, fancy pattern

F. Kui poepoe, double, ½ crown, rickrack lei, circular pattern

G. Kui poepoe, double, ⅕ crown, rickrack lei, circular pattern

ʻIlima Lei

The ʻilima lei is made from delicate, tissue paper-like flowers, yellow to deep gold in color, 1" in diameter with five petals; no fragrance.

Lei Characteristics: The ʻilima is the flower of Oʻahu; a lei of royalty; fragile and lasts one day.

Season/Harvest Period: Year-round, peaking in the summer. To prevent bruising, pick in bud form before sunrise, no later than early mid-morning. Flowers open to full bloom by noon.

Storage: Keep dry and airtight. Wrap in dry tissue or a paper towel. Place in a plastic container or bag. Refrigerate.

Materials

- Thin or medium 8" lei needle
- 52" length, carpet thread, glace finish, cotton covered polyester. Tie a double knot about 6" from one end of the string. Hook on the lei needle.
- A flat sheet of Styrofoam board.

Quantity

- 650 to 700 blossoms for a 40" single, kui pololei, straight pattern.

1. Pick blossoms in the bud stage. Let sit for 2 hours for blossoms to open.

2. Pinch off calyx. Place blossoms face down on a Styrofoam sheet.

3. Pierce about 15 blossoms using a Styrofoam sheet as a base. Gently hold blossoms and pull down to knotted end of string. Continue until 40" long.

'Ilima Lei Patterns

A. Kui pololei, single lei, straight pattern
B. Kui pololei wili, straight single pattern, twisting 2 strands

Orchid (Dendrobium)

Orchid lei are ubiquitous in the islands these days—more so than plumeria.

Lei Characteristics: Orchids are hardy, long-lasting, and have a tropical allure; available in white, lavender, purple, green, and brown; popular for shipping to the mainland; lasts three to four days. Dendrobium orchid plants require a tropical, warm climate; backyard cultivation; indirect or direct sunlight.

Season/Harvest Period: Year-round, however some varieties do not blossom in quantity December through February. Pick when blossoms are fully open and when cool.

Storage: Sprinkle lightly with water. Place in a plastic bag or container. Refrigerate. May be revived by soaking in cold water in the refrigerator for 4 hours. Shake off excess water. Place in a plastic bag and refrigerate.

Materials

- Medium 12" lei needle
- 104" length 3-ply lei twine or 10# crochet thread, folded in half. Tie a double knot about 6" from open end of the string. Hook on the lei needle.

Quantity

- 50 blossoms for a 40" single lei, kui pololei, straight pattern
- 110-120 blossoms for a 40" double lei, kui poepoe, circular pattern
- 530 blossoms (lips only) for a 40" flat lei, kui lau, back-and-forth "Christina" pattern
- 1,200 blossoms (dorsal sepals only) for a 40" double-sepal lei, kui poepoe, circular "Robyn" pattern
- 750-765 blossoms=1,500-1,530 (petals only) for a 40" double-petal patterned lei, kui poepoe circular "Keali'i I" pattern
- 425 (lips only) for a 40" double-lip lei, kui poepoe, circular "Keali'i II" pattern

Note: There are more than 700 varieties of dendrobium orchids.

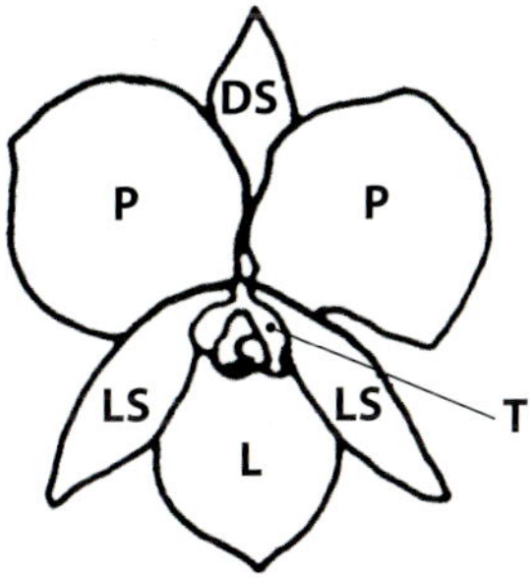

The parts of a dendrobium orchid: **DS**=dorsal sepals, **P**=petals, **C**=column or nose, **T**=throat, **LS**=lateral sepals, **L**=lips

2. Pierce about 6 blossoms, placing 3 in a circular pattern for a double lei. Pierce laterally through backs. Gently pull the blossoms down to the knotted end of the string. Continue until lei is 40" long (see Figure B on p.14).

4. Pull off the top sepal for a double-sepal lei, also known as a "Robyn" lei.

1. Pierce about 3 blossoms for a single lei; pierce from the nose and through the throat. Gently pull down to knotted end of the string. Continue until 40" long (see Figure A on p. 14).

3. Pierce about 10 blossoms, placing the lips in a back-and-forth pattern for a "Christina" or flat lei. Gently pull the lips down to the knotted end of the string. Continue until the lei is 40" long (see Figure C on p. 14).

5. Pierce about 35 sepals, placing 7 in a circular pattern. Gently pull sepals down to knotted end of the string. Continue until the lei is 40" long (see Figure D on p. 14).

6. Pull off the petals for a double-petal patterned lei; also known as a "Keali'i I" lei. Pierce a stack of 10 petals, placing 5 stacks in a circular pattern. Gently pull petals down to the knotted end of the string. Continue until 40" long (see Figure E).

7. Pull off the lips for a double-lip lei; also known as a "Keali'i II" lei. Fold down the right side of the lip. Pierce 12 lips in a circular pattern. Gently pull lips down to the knotted end of the string. Continue until 40" long (see Figure F).

A→
B→
C→
D→
E→
F→

Orchid Lei Patterns

A. Kui pololei, single lei, straight pattern
B. Kui poepoe, double lei, circular pattern
C. Kui lau, flat lei, "Christina," back-and-forth pattern
D. Kui poepoe, double-sepal "Robyn" lei, circular pattern
E. Kui poepoe, double petal pattern lei, "Keali'i I," circular pattern
F. Kui poepoe, double lip lei, "Keali'i II," circular pattern

Pīkake Lei

Pīkake, or Arabian Jasmine, is a shrub with small, white, tubular, pearl-like 3/4" long buds. The fully-open flowers are about 1" in diameter; 5-9 petals; intensely fragrant.

Lei Characteristics: Pīkake is a popular wedding flower lei in Hawai'i. The buds start to blossom immediately when not refrigerated. Lei lasts for one day.

Season/Harvest Period: Year-round. Low in the months of December through February. Pick early in the morning as buds. Place in a sealed glass jar. Refrigerate until enough buds have been collected.

Storage: Keep dry. Coil up in a flat spiral pattern. Wrap in waxed paper. Refrigerate.

Materials

- Medium 12" lei needle
- 104" length 3-ply lei twine or #10 crochet thread, folded in half. Tie a double knot about 6" from the open end of the string. Hook on the lei needle.

Quantity

- 90-105 blossoms for a 40" single lei, kui pololei, straight pattern
- 530-630 blossoms for a 40" small double lei, 25 cent coin size, kui poepoe, circular pattern
- 800-900 blossoms for a 40" medium double lei, 50 cent coin size, kui poepoe, circular pattern
- 950-1,000 blossoms for a 40" large double lei, silver dollar coin size, kui poepoe, circular pattern

1. Pierce about 5 blossoms for a single lei. Gently hold blossoms and pull down to the knotted end of the string. Continue until lei is 40" long (see Figure A on p. 16).

2. Pierce about 50 blossoms, placing 4 in a circular pattern, for a double lei, or a small rope lei (see Figure B). Place 6 in a circular pattern for a double lei, or medium rope lei (see Figure C). Place 7 in a circular pattern for a double lei, or large rope lei (see Figure D). Gently hold blossoms and pull down to the knotted end of the string. Continue until lei is 40" long.

A→
B→
C→
D→

Pikake Lei Patterns

A. Kui pololei single lei, straight pattern
B. Kui poepoe, small double or small rope, circular pattern
C. Kui poepoe, medium double lei or medium rope, circular pattern
D. Kui poepoe, large double lei or large rope, circular pattern

Plumeria Lei

Plumeria trees have five-petal blossoms about 2" in diameter that are very fragrant; many color variations.

Lei Characteristics: Plumeria lei last only one to two days. The milky sap is poisonous if ingested.

Season/Harvest Period: Grows in warm climate; backyard cultivation; low elevation; direct sunlight. Dormant during the winter, peaking March through November.

Storage: Sprinkle lightly with water. Wrap in damp paper or a cloth towel. Place in the sink or a bowl. Keep cool; do not refrigerate.

Materials

- Thick 12" lei needle
- 101" length 3-ply lei twine or #10 crochet thread, folded in half. Tie a double knot about 6" from the open end of the string. Hook on the lei needle.

Quantity

- 50-60 blossoms for a 40" single lei, kui pololei, straight pattern
- 110-120 blossoms for a 40" double lei, kui poepoe, circular pattern.

1. Pierce about 4 blossom for a single lei. Gently hold blossoms and pull down to the knotted end of string. Continue until the lei is 40" long (see Figure A).

2. Pierce 3 blossoms in a circular pattern for a double lei.

3. Pierce about 9 blossoms. Gently hold blossoms and pull down to knotted end of string. Continue until 40" long (see Figure B).

Plumeria Lei Patterns

A

B

Pua Kenikeni Lei

Pua Kenikeni trees produce 2" long, 5-petal white tubular blossoms that change to yellow then orange and have a strong perfume fragrance.

Lei Characteristics: The flower has been called the "ten-cent flower" since Hawai'i's Boat Days of the 1800s and early 1900s. It is rumored that the blossoms were so prized, a pua kenikeni lei sold for ten cents. The lei lasts for three days.

Season/Harvest Period: Grows in warm climate; backyard cultivation; direct sunlight. Seasonal from April through November. Pick the blossoms in the early morning or evening when cool.

Storage: Keep dry and cool. Place in an air-filled plastic bag; float the bag with lei in a container of water; keep at room temperature; do not refrigerate.

Materials

- Thick 12" lei needle
- 104" length knitting yarn, folded in half, for a kui pololei, single lei
- 104" length 3-ply lei twine or #10 crochet thread for a double lei, kui poepoe, circular pattern. Tie a double knot about 6" from one end of the string. Hook on the lei needle.

Quantity

- 45 blossoms for a 40" single lei, kui pololei, straight pattern
- 100 blossoms for a 40" double lei, kui poepoe, circular pattern

Note: You may also use a strip of a sheet or cotton fabric for thread in a single lei, kui pololei straight pattern.

1. Cut off the calyx, leaving a 1" corolla.

2. Pierce about 5 blossoms. Gently hold the blossoms and pull down to the knotted end of the string. Continue until lei is 40" long (see Figure A).

3. Cut the calyx, leaving a 3/4" corolla. Pierce about 9 blossoms, placing 3 in a circular pattern for a double lei. Gently hold the blossoms and pull down to knotted end of string. Continue until lei is 40" long (see Figure B).

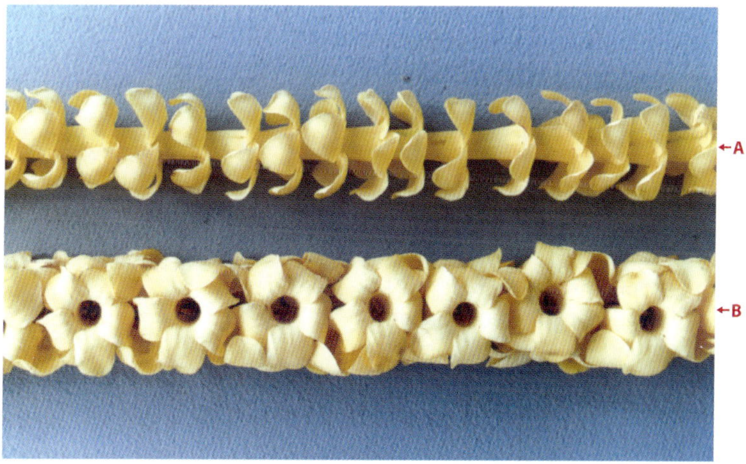

Pua Kenikeni Lei Patterns

A. Kui pololei, single lei, straight pattern
B. Kui poepoe, double lei, circular pattern

Rose Lei

The rose, or loke, bush bears 1" long rose buds that have a light fragrance when they blossom.

Lei Characteristics: Loke blossom leaves may carry microscopic insect pets. The Federal Department of Agriculture prohibits this flower, with its leaves, to be taken to the mainland. The flower buds are not prohibited. The lei lasts two to three days.

Season/Harvest Period: Grows in a tropical, warm climate; backyard cultivation; direct sunlight. Year-round, peaking in summer. Pick blossoms early in the morning when in the tight bud stage.

Storage: Keep lei in a damp paper towel. Place in plastic bag or container; refrigerate.

Materials

- Medium 12" lei needle
- 104" length 3-ply lei twine or #10 crochet thread, folded in half. Tie a double knot about 6" from the open end of the string. Hook on the lei needle.

Quantity

- 40 blossoms for a 40" single lei, kui pololei, straight pattern
- 175 blossoms for a double lei, kui poepoe, double lei, circular pattern

1. Break off the stems of the blossoms.

2. Pierce about 4 blossoms. Gently hold the blossoms and pull down to the knotted end of the string. Continue until lei is 40" long (see Figure A).

2. Pierce about 6 blossoms, placing 3 in a circular pattern for a double lei. Gently hold the blossoms and pull down to the knotted end of the string. Continue until lei is 40" long (see Figure B).

←A

←B

Rose Lei Patterns

A. Kui pololei, single lei, straight pattern

B. Kui poepoe, double lei, circular pattern

Ti Leaf Lei

The ti plant has narrow, oblong, smooth, shiny, flexible leaves 1-2' long and approximately 4" wide that grow in spiral clusters.

Lei Characteristics: Plant and leaves are believed to ward off evil spirits and bring good luck. Lei lasts five to seven days; also used as a dried lei.

Season/Harvest Period: Grows in a warm climate; backyard cultivation; direct or indirect sunlight. Year-round. Pick the mature leaves and harvest any time.

Storage: Keep dry. Wrap in newspaper and refrigerate.

Materials

- Scissors
- Microwave oven or iron

Quantity

- 5 to 7 large leaves for a 50" single lei, wili, winding, twisting pattern
- 12-13 large leaves for a 60" Maile style lei, wili, winding, twisting pattern
- 8-10 large leaves for a 40" orchid, wili, winding, twisting pattern

1. Wipe leaves. Cut out the spines of about 7 leaves. Cut the leaves into fourths, at a 45° angle. Keep one full half of a leaf. Microwave the segments for one minute to make them pliable. (Or, freeze and iron leaves or dip them in hot water to soften them.)

2. Tie a knot to join one long and one short leaf segment, about 1" from top.

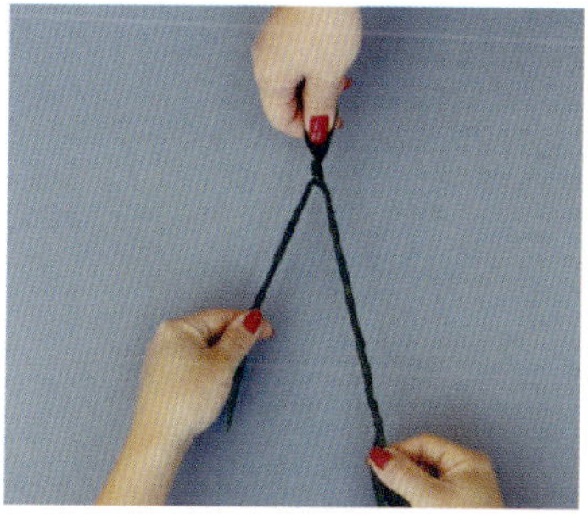

3. Twist both sides to the right, in the same direction.

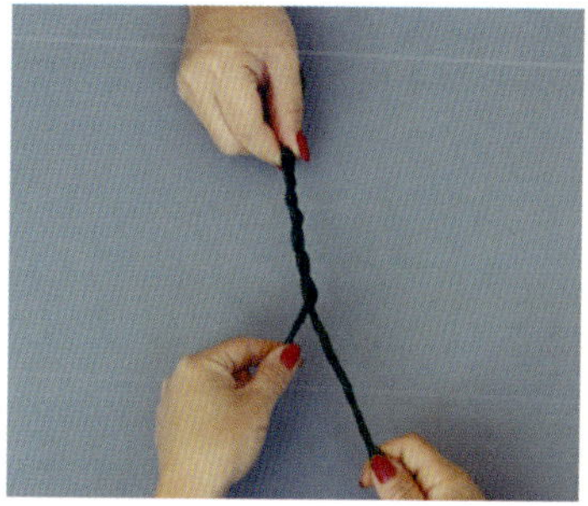

4. Evenly twist both sides with each other by always crossing the right side over the left. Lengthen by twisting in a new leaf segment, placing it 1½" above the twisting point.

5. Twist in with the shorter side of the lei. Keep twisting and adding until 45" long. Tie a knot to end lei. Trim leaf points to create a leaf-like pattern (see Figure B on p. 24).

6. Cut 14 long, full-length segments and 65 short, 5" segments, totaling 14 leaves for a Maile style lei (see Figure A on p. 24. Tie a knot 1" from the end, joining 2 long segments. Twist both sides to the right. Twine both sides with each other, crossing the right side over the left. Twine 2 times. Add a leaf segment.

7. Add another small leaf segment and twist twice. Twist in the new long segments as twining leaves become short. Continue until 80" long. Knot the end.

9. Add an orchid. Twine one, then add a leaf segment. Keep twisting both hands to the right at all times. Twine 3 times, then add an orchid. Twine once, then add a leaf segment. Continue the twisting and twining pattern until lei is 40" long. Knot the end.

8. Cut 16 long segments and 22 short, 3" triangles totaling 10 large leaves for a ti leaf orchid lei (see Figure C). Cut the same amount of triangles as orchids; a minimum of 8 orchids per lei is recommended. Tie a knot 1" from the end, join the 2 leaves. Twist both sides to the right. Twine both sides with each other, crossing right over left. Twine 3 times.

Ti Leaf Lei Patterns

A. Wili, Maile style lei, winding, twisting pattern
B. Wili, single lei, winding, twisting pattern
C. Wili, orchid lei, winding, twisting pattern

Tuberose Lei

Tuberose plants have grass-like leaves and 2" elongated white blossoms with spreading, oblong petals; strong fragrance.

Lei Characteristics: Popular among visitors for its fragrance. The lei lasts one to two days.

Season/Harvest Period: Grows in a warm climate; backyard cultivation; direct sunlight. Year-round. Pick the fully-opened blossoms in the morning or evening when it is cool.

Storage: Keep dry. Place in paper bag and refrigerate.

Materials

- Medium 12" lei needle
- 104" long 3-ply twine or #10 crochet thread, folded in half. Tie a double knot about 6" from the open end of the string. Hook on the lei needle.

Quantity

- Approximately 30-45 blossoms for a single lei, kui pololei, straight pattern
- 150-160 blossoms for a double lei, kui poepoe, circular pattern

1. Pinch off the calyx along with ¼" of the corolla. The shorter the corolla, the more blossoms needed to make a 40" long lei.

2. Peel off the outer damaged petals if necessary.

3. Pierce about 5 blossoms, starting at the base end, for a single lei. Gently pull the blossoms down to the knotted end of the string. Continue until lei is 40" long (see Figure A).

4. Pierce about 12 blossoms, placing 3 in a circular pattern for a double lei. Gently hold the blossoms and pull down to the knotted end of the string. Continue until lei is 40" long (see Figure B).

A→

B→

Tuberose Lei Patterns

A. Kui pololei, single lei, straight pattern
B. Kui poepoe, double lei, circular pattern

Crochet Lei

Making Crochet Lei

Crochet lei making is also very popular in Hawai'i—the lei are fairly easy and quick to make, even for beginners. Two basic stitches are used—the single crochet and the chain stitch. Practice with a simple, clean yarn and you'll be surprised how easy it is. There's no wrong way to make a lei. Every lei is different because every person making it is different. Let your personality come through, and have fun. Change the color of the yarns to fit your vision of the lei. For the Graduation Lei (see p. 52) choose your school colors and you'll have a memento that will be treasured forever.

It's amazing what you can do with ribbons and yarns. There is an incredibly wide variety on the market today. Just to name a few types of yarns, there's boa, eyebrow, eyelash, fizz, mustache or mustachio. These yarns are available at any craft store or online. Match the color of the lei to the flower you're creating to make it look more natural, or experiment and create a new style of lei.

Just like the yarns, there are different sizes and types of ribbons. Satin or grosgrain ribbon can be used. The ⅛" satin ribbon works well for lead lines (lines you crochet on) and ⅝" satin ribbon works well for ending the lei.

The most popular length is a short choker, which measures about 36-38" (120 loops). For lei po'o or head lei, measurements differ depending on head size. The lei po'o (125 to 130 loops) can also be used on a hat. The normal lei length measures 38 to 42 inches (250 to 300 loops).

Kukui nuts are the basic nuts used to secure lei when ending it, but you can use any variety of nuts to secure your lei, like sheep's eye, ironwood, Hawaiian gray pearl, and the blue marble. It just depends on how you want your final lei to look.

Don't worry about making mistakes. Everyone does, and it may not be noticeable; but if it is, just take it apart and correct it. Keep in mind that even the best crocheters may not notice it. The aloha you put into making the lei is much more important than how perfect the finished product it.

Document your steps in making a lei—especially ones you create yourself. Someone may want you to make a second lei, and this way you'll know what color yarns and ribbons you used. Keep a strand of each in a labeled bag or envelope, or keep the label from the yarns so you have something to refer to.

Most of all, have fun, be creative, and be generous. A lei—whether it's made with flowers or with yarn and ribbon—is always made with aloha and should be given to and shared with others.

Supplies

Crochet hook: I like to use the "J" hook, but it depends if your hand is tight or loose. If your hand is tight, then it's best if you use a larger needle. If your hand is loose, then you should use a smaller needle. Try both, if you can, and see which feels more comfortable to you.

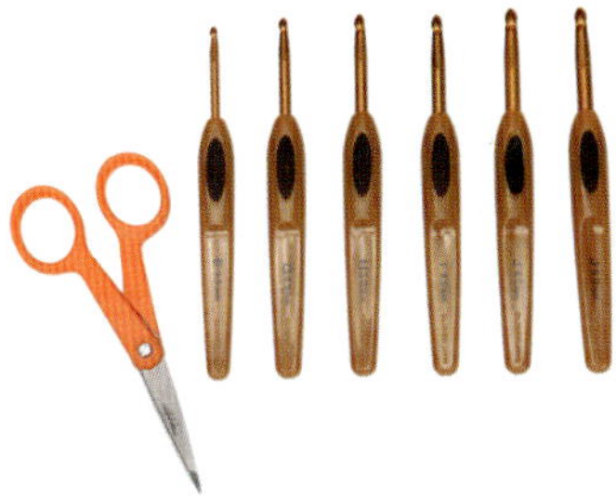

Ribbons: You can use satin or grosgrain ribbon. Use ⅛" satin ribbon for making rosettes and pīkake and ⅝" satin ribbon for ending the lei. Follow instructions on what kind and size ribbon for each lei.

Yarns: There are so many different kinds of yarns for you to use and experiment with. Just to name a few there's: funny yarn (eyebrow), fizz (whiskers), peluche (mustache), salsa (eyebrow), and boa. When beginning, just pick up the type you need. After you've made a few lei and feel comfortable, experiment and see what you come up with by using different types of yarn. Pretty soon you'll be an expert and will know the difference between a fizz yarn and a boa yarn.

Crocheting is a very simple art—not only in how it is done, but what is needed. Basically, all you need is a needle and some yarn.

Locally, supplies can be found at craft stores throughout the islands. Any department store that carries crafts may also carry yarns. The internet is also a great resource.

Measurements vary depending on what type of lei you want to make, so in terms of how much yarn or ribbon to purchase, start with one ball of each. Two to three lei can be made from each ball of yarn or ribbon. As you make the different lei, you will begin to collect different colors and types of yarns and ribbons. Use your leftovers to create different colored lei. Although it may seem the supplies are expensive, remember that a number of lei can be made from one roll.

Basic Stitches and Patterns

Chain Stitch

This is a basic crochet stitch that creates a chain of loops. This chain can be used as the first row of your lei—the foundation upon which other rows are built.

1. Draw up a loop with your yarn.

2. Pull your needle through the loop.

3. Hook the side of the yarn with your needle.

4. Pull the yarn through the loop.

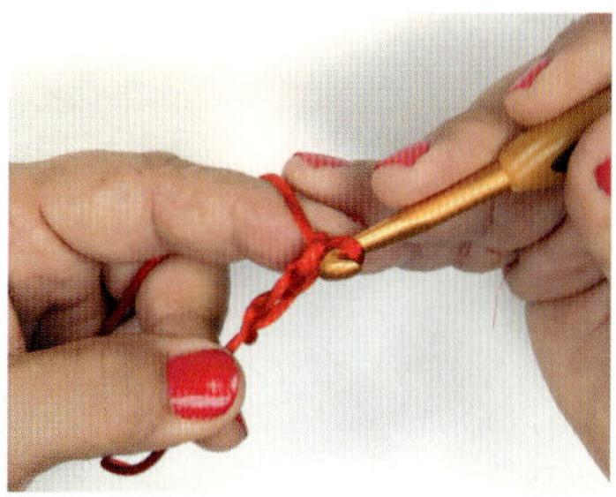

5. Repeat the previous steps to create a chain of yarn.

Single Crochet Stitch

This is a basic crochet stitch that is built on a foundation of chains or a lead line of ribbon.

1. Make a foundation row of chains or use your lead line of ribbon.
2. Insert hook through the first chain (if using ribbon: ribbon over hook).

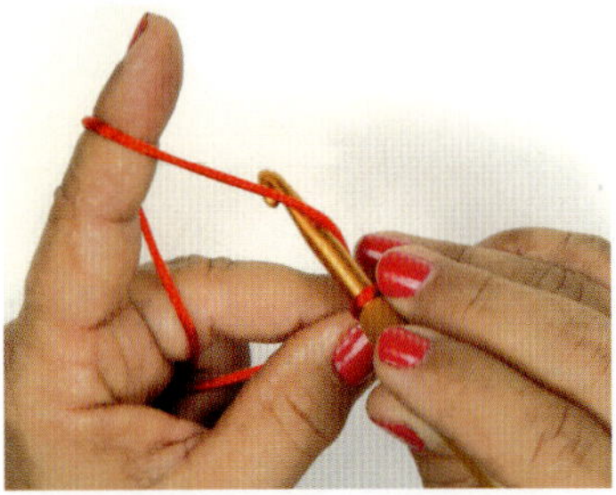

3. Yarn over hook.

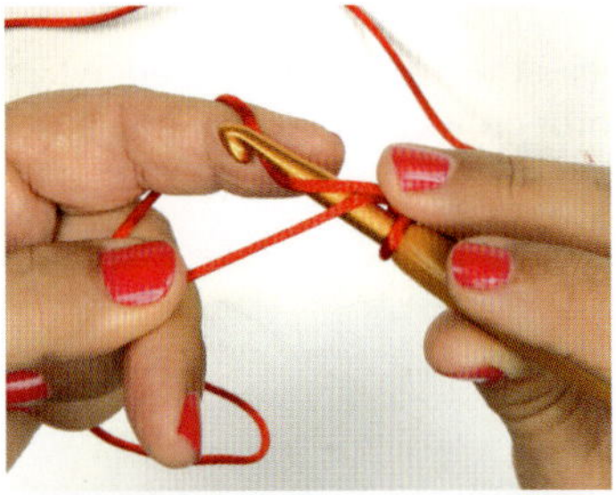

4. Pull through the first chain. If using ribbon, pull hook under the ribbon.

5. There will be two loops of yarn on your hook.

6. Yarn over and pull through the two loops.

Lead Line

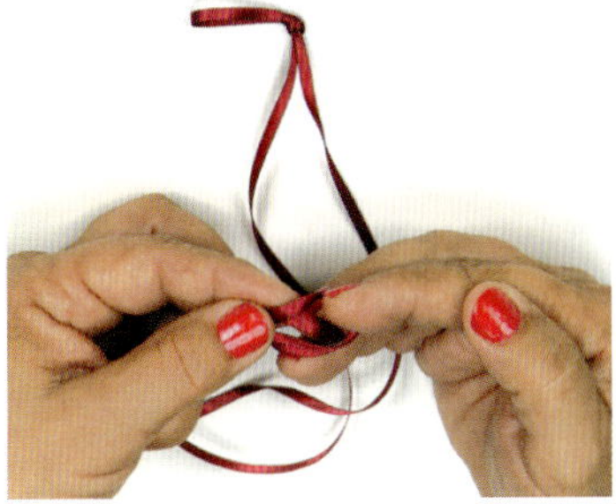

To begin your lei, you need a lead line. You can make lei any length you choose, but the two common lengths are the choker length and the regular length.

For a choker length lei: Measure ⅛" ribbon (any color will do) about 60". Fold the ribbon in half (30"), then tie a knot at both ends to secure the lei from sliding off the line.

For regular length lei: Measure ⅛" ribbon (any color will do) about 100 inches. Fold the ribbon in half (50"), then tie a knot at both ends to secure the lei from sliding off the line.

Crochet Lei Pattern #1

Supplies needed

See the instructions starting on page 51 for supplies specific to the lei you choose.

1. Make a loop with your yarn.

2. Pull the yarn through the loop.

3. Take your lead line (see p. 33) and single crochet in between ribbons, then chain 3.

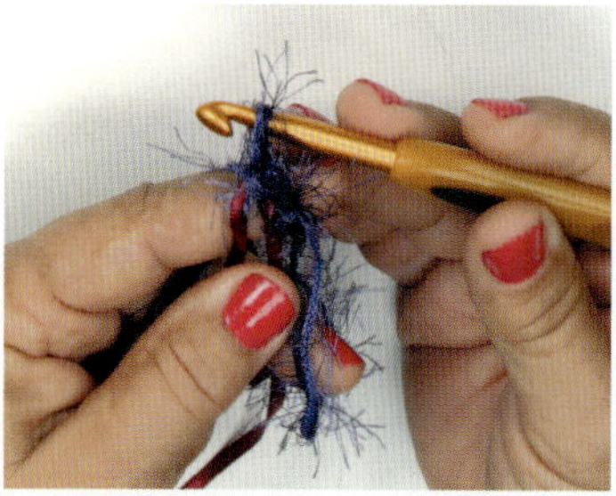

4. First Row: Single crochet both ribbons together, then chain 3, and repeat until you have 125 loops. This is your first row. Single crochet into the last single crochet and do one more chain, pull through chain, and cut off threads.

5a. Second Row: Single crochet both ribbons together. Chain 3 in between loops.

5b. Repeat until the end of the row and end as row 1.

6a. Single crochet both ribbons together and chain 3.

6b. Push first and second single crochet to the right and single crochet, then chain 3 next to second single crochet. Repeat until the end of the row. End row same as rows 1 and 2.

7. Pull threads down to one end making sure you do not make it tight or your lei will look crooked. Tie the other end close to the first stitches.

Crochet Lei Pattern #2

Supplies needed

- Two skeins of main color (Blue boa)
- One skein of second color (White boa)
- J hook

Graduation Lei

Choose the colors of your school and use any type of yarn. I prefer splash or boa to get the satin lei look.

- First color: Single crochet and chain 3 fifty times, then cut off thread.
- Second color: Single crochet and chain 3 twenty-five times, then cut off thread.

Repeat until length has been reached. Make 10 first color sections and 10 second color sections. End by tying lei together and add a bow.

This is one of the easiest lei to make. Use two colors of yarn one strand at a time. There are so many designs you can make.

1. Take your lead line (see p.33) and follow Crochet Lei Pattern #1steps 1 and 2. Then single crochet.

2. Chain 3. Repeat until you have 50 loops.

3. Snip off the yarn.

4. Attach a white or second color yarn.

5. Single crochet and chain 3. Repeat until you have 25 loops.

6. Repeat, alternating blue and white yarn until you reach your desired length.

7. Tie the completed lei together. Add a bow where the ends join.

Crochet Lei Pattern #3

Supplies needed

- Dark Blue ⅛" ribbon
- Medium Blue ⅛" ribbon
- Light Blue ⅛" ribbon
- Olive eyebrow
- Sherbet (fizz) whiskers
- J hook

Rosettes or Pīkake

See the instructions starting on page 51 for supplies specific to the lei you choose.

Measure 60" of ⅛" ribbon (for choker), fold in half as in lei pattern #1. Tie both ends with a knot.

1. First Row: Using your first two threads, single crochet in between ⅛" ribbons, chain 3.

2. Single crochet, then chain 3 on line making sure you have 125 loops for choker-length, longer if making a regular lei.

3. Second Row: Single crochet in between loops picking up both ribbons. Chain 4 and single crochet in third chain from hook, single crochet in last chain, then chain 2.

4. Single crochet, then chain 4. Then single crochet in third chain from hook. Single crochet in last chain, then chain 2. Repeat between loops. This will make 125 rosettes.

5. Third Row: Using the first color ribbon, single crochet between loops and follow instructions for First Row.

6. Chain 4 and single crochet in third chain from hook. Then single crochet in last chain.

7. Continue in between loops. Be sure to push greens and first ribbon to the right.

8. Fourth Row: Using the second color ribbon, push 2 single crochet to the right.

9. Single crochet and chain 3 next to second single crochet—follow directions for Row Two to make rosettes.

10. Repeat until the end of the row. If you want to make a pīkake lei, use ⅛" ribbon or off-white ⅛" ribbon for all three rows or mix it with other color rosettes. To finish your lei, see p. 47.

Crochet Lei Pattern #4

Supplies needed

- Red rattail cord
- Red shiny cellophane yarn
- J hook

See the instructions starting on page 51 for supplies specific to the lei you choose.

1. Take one strand of Rattail together with one strand of yarn.

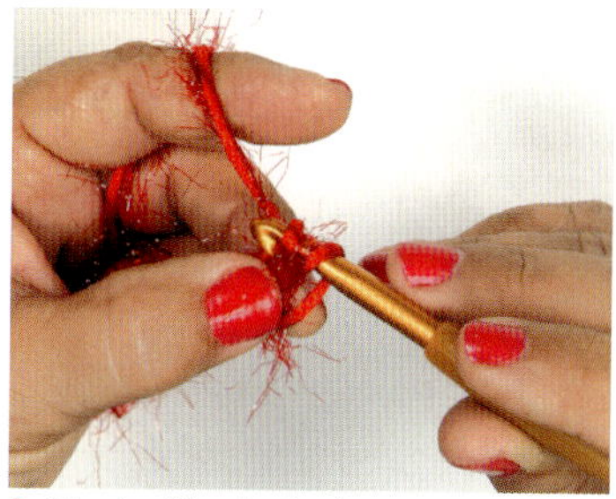

2. Start with chain 4.

3. Chain 4.

4. Insert needle through first chain.

5. Pull strands through both loops to form a ring (circle). Slip stitch is complete.

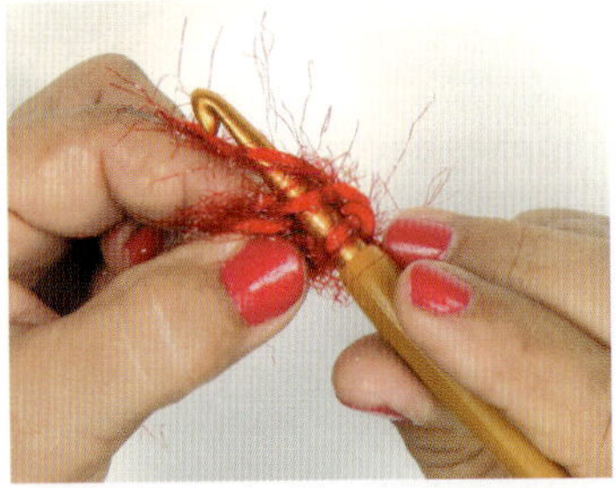

6. Single crochet in each chain around the ring (circle).

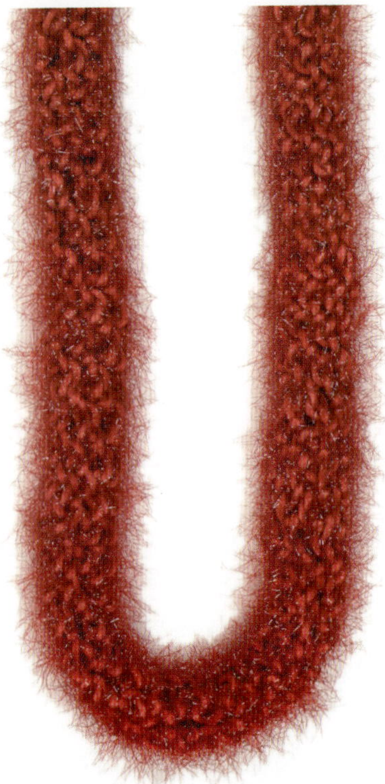

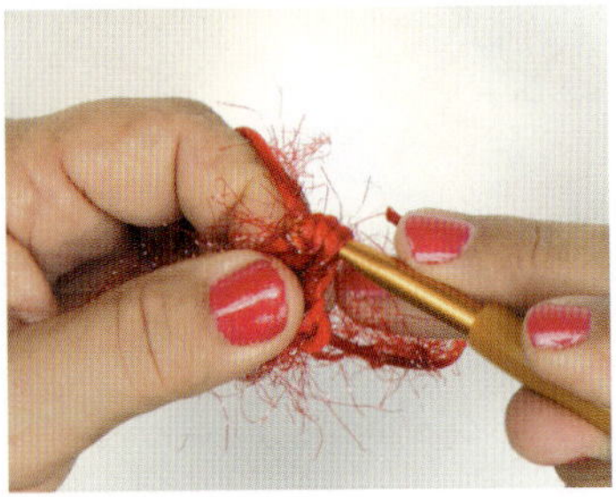

7. Continue around until the lei is the length you want. For a regular lei, length should be 36 to 40".

8. See Securing Your Lei on p. 48 to complete the lei.

Crochet Lei Pattern #5

Supplies needed

- 1½ yards of ⅝" black satin ribbon
- J hook

1. Your satin ribbon is your lead line. Starting with brown yarn, single crochet and chain 3 five times and cut off yarn.

2. Using yellow yarn, single crochet and chain 5 times and cut off yarn. Repeat until desired length.

Crochet Lei Pattern #6

Supplies needed

- 200–300 beads
- Big-eyed sewing needle
- ⅛" satin ribbon
- 2 different kinds or colors of eyelash

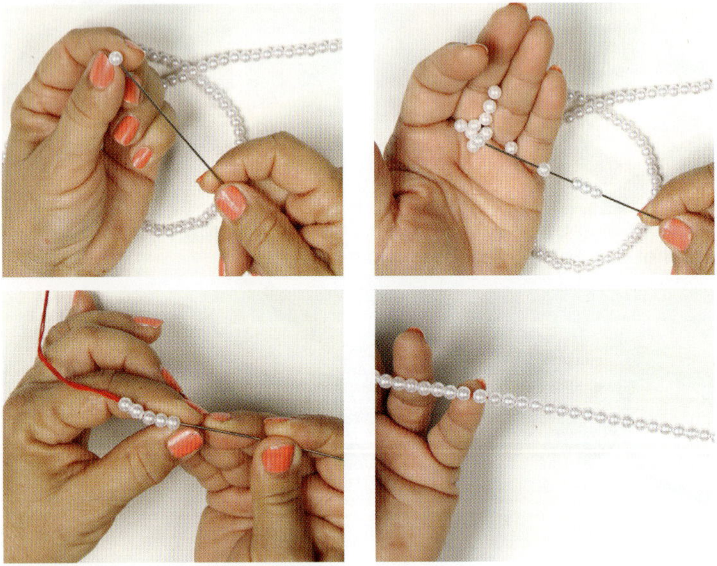

1. String beads on ⅛" ribbon (use a needle that goes through beads).

2. Using lead line to work on, start with both colors of eyelash together, single crochet and chain. Continue until you get your desired length.

3. Using the beads on the ribbon, single crochet chain 2. Pull up a bead and chain 2, then single crochet between chain 3 stitches on first row. Continue until end. See p. 48 to secure the lei.

Crochet Lei Pattern #7

Supplies needed

- White boa, double strand
- Purple mix boa, single strand
- J hook

1. Chain 4, slip stitch in first chain. Start with chain 4.

2. Chain 4, single crochet in next loop.

3. Turn, repeat until 34" in length is done, then cut off yarn.

4. Add purple yarn to right side.

5. Single crochet chain 2 and single crochet in next loop on side of lei. Repeat around lei cut-off. If your lei does not lie flat, you need to slip stitch in center of lei, then end lei. See steps below to finish the lei.

Finishing Your Lei

These instructions show you how to finish your lei. This is applicable to all patterns.

After twisting your lei, you can fluff it so it looks fuller. Just take your lei and shake it. This can be done at anytime.

1. Take the middle of the lei in your left hand and twist the right side with your right hand going clockwise.

2. Then turn the lei, take the right side in your left hand, and do the same as in step 1.

3. To tie off your ends, take the two yarns and tie a knot. Take the next two yarns and tie a knot. Do the same for the last two yarns and cut off ends as close to stitches as possible. This prevents your lei from accidentally coming apart.

Securing Your Lei

Supplies needed

- 2 kukui nuts (color of your choice)
- ⅝" satin or grosgrain ribbon
- 15" needle and thread
- Big-eyed needle
- Pair of pliers (optional)
- Clean nail polish

These instructions show you how to finish and secure your lei so that it looks tidy and won't fall apart.

1. Push back stitches on lei until you have 2 inches of line you crocheted on.

2. Split ribbons to make an opening.

3. Take ⅝" ribbon and pull through opening.

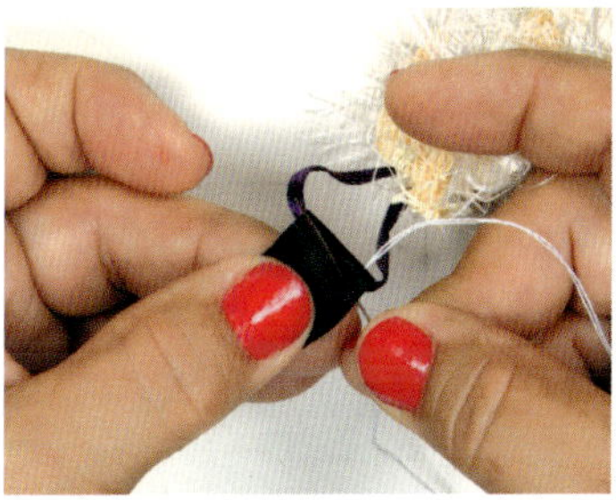

4. Fold edge of ribbon slightly.

5. Put a few hand stitches through ribbon to secure the lei.

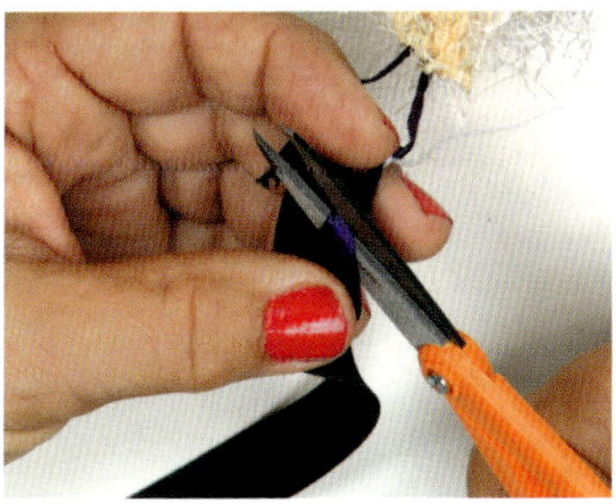

6. Trim the short end of the ribbon after sewing.

7. Put kukui nut on ribbon. If you use a big needle, it may fit through the kukui nut. If not, use pliers to pull the needle through. There's no right or wrong way (top or bottom) for you to put your kukui nut on the ribbon.

8. Push the thread and adjust the lei down to both ends after the kukui nut is on. Tie a knot at the end of the nut to secure it in place (both ends).

9. This secures the nut. Do this to both ends of the lei. Go back to Step 1 and repeat on the other end of the lei.

10. Snip the ribbon at both ends of the lei.

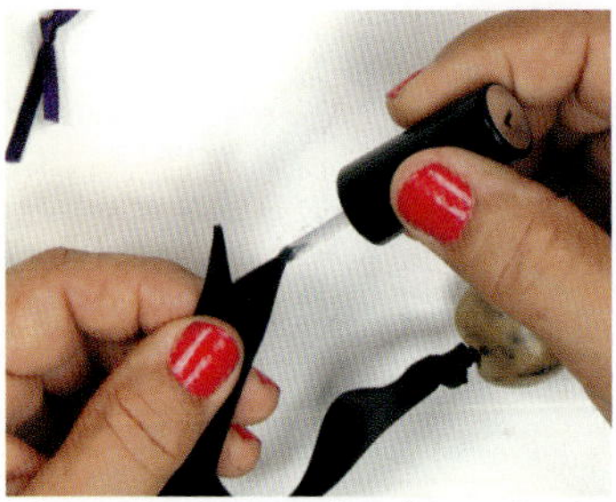

11. Apply clear nail polish so that the ribbon does not fray, then tie the two ribbons together to close the lei.

Crochet Lei Instructions

Cigar Lei

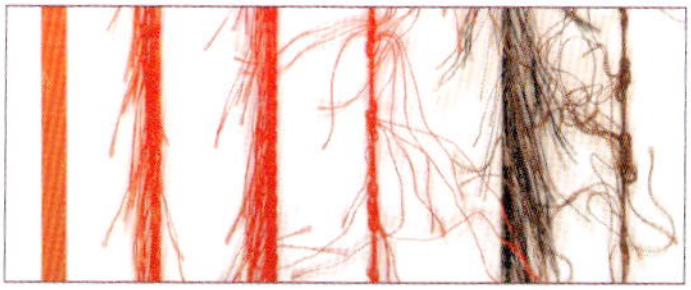

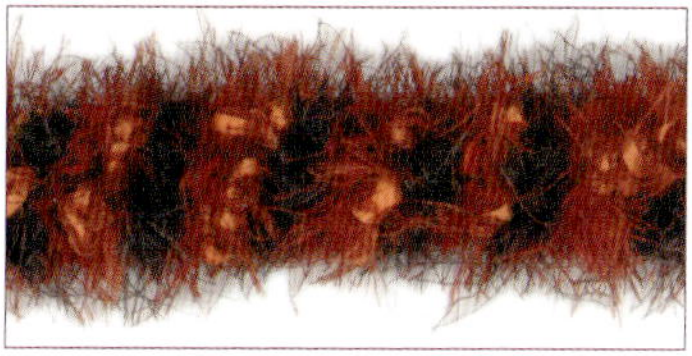

Supplies needed

- Orange ⅛" ribbon
- Rust eyebrow
- Red eyebrow
- Flame (fizz) whiskers
- Brown & Tan mix mustache
- Brown (fizz) whiskers

Instructions

Follow instructions for Lei Pattern #1 on p. 33.

Row 1. Orange ribbon with Rust eyebrow.

Row 2. Red eyebrow with Flame (fizz) whiskers.

Row 3. Brown & Tan mix mustache with Brown (fizz) whiskers.

Graduation Lei

Supplies needed

- 2 (primary color of school) boa
- 1 (secondary color of school) boa
- (Refer to p. 132 for Hawai'i high school and college/university colors)

Instructions

Follow instructions for Lei Pattern #2 on p. 36.

Row 1. First color 50 loops.
Row 2. Second color 25 loops.

ʻŌhai Aliʻi with Yellow Lehua

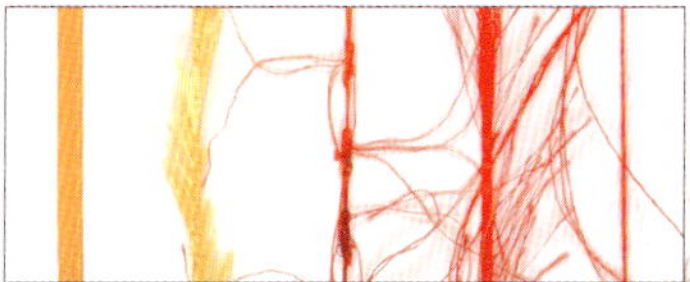

Supplies needed

- Yellow ⅛" ribbon
- Yellow eyebrow
- Flame (fizz) whiskers
- Red eyebrow
- Red eyelash

Instructions

Follow instructions for Lei Pattern #4 on 41.

Row 1. Yellow ⅛" ribbon with Yellow eyebrow.
Row 2. Flame (fizz) whiskers with Red eyebrow.
Row 3. Flame (fizz) whiskers with Red eyelash.

Mixed Rosettes

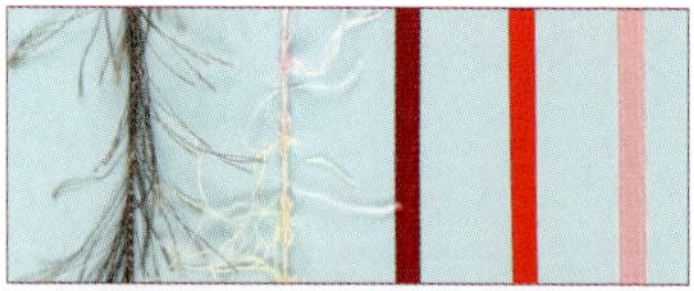

Supplies needed

- Olive eyebrow
- Sherbet (fizz) whisker
- Maroon ⅛" ribbon
- Red ⅛" ribbon
- Pink ⅛" ribbon
- (Or, colors of your choice)

Instructions

Follow instructions for Lei Pattern #3 on 38.

Row 1. Olive eyebrow with Sherbet (fizz) whiskers.
Row 2. Maroon ⅛" ribbon.
Row 3. Red ⅛" ribbon.
Row 4. Pink ⅛" ribbon.

Hinahina

Supplied needed

- Green Aquarius
- Olive ⅛" ribbon
- Pele's hair (fizz)
- Gray ⅛" ribbon
- Black Aquarius

Instructions

Follow instructions for Lei Pattern #1 on p. 33.

Row 1. Green Aquarius with Olive ⅛" ribbon.
Row 2. Pele's hair (fizz) with Gray ⅛" ribbon.
Row 3. Pele's hair (fizz) with Black Aquarius.

Mokihana

Supplies needed

- Olive ⅛" ribbon
- Green carisso
- Olive eyebrow
- Olive mustache
- Lettuce (fizz) whiskers

Instructions

Follow instructions for Lei Pattern #1 on p. 33.

Row 1. Olive ⅛" ribbon with Green carisso.

Row 2. Olive eyebrow with Olive mustache.

Row 3. Olive mustache with Lettuce (fizz) whiskers.

Ōla'a Beauty

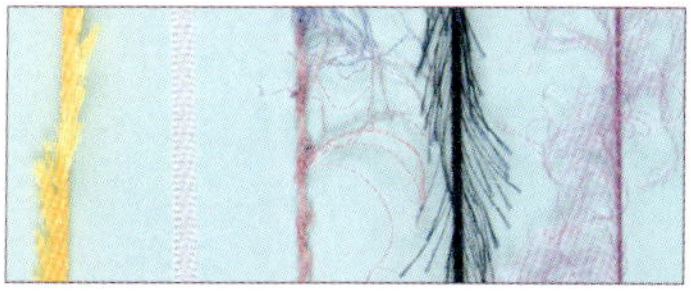

Supplies needed

- Yellow mustache
- White ⅛" ribbon
- Delphinium (fizz) whiskers
- Navy eyebrow
- Purple viola

Instructions

Follow instructions for Lei Pattern #3 on p. 38.

Row 1. Yellow mustache with White 18" ribbon.
Row 2. Purple viola with Navy eyebrow.
Row 3. Navy eyebrow with Delphinium (fizz) whiskers.

Red & Yellow Lehua

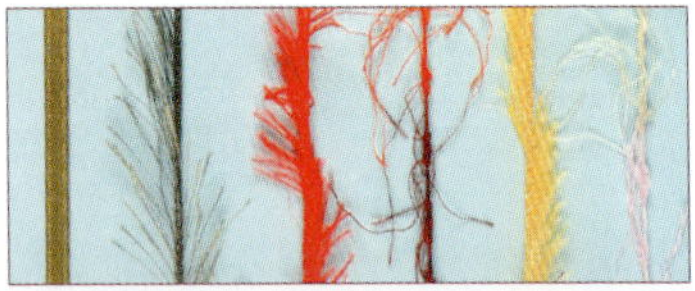

Supplies needed

- Olive ⅛" ribbon
- Olive mustache
- Red mustache
- Flame (fizz) whiskers
- Yellow mustache
- Sherbet (fizz) whiskers

Instructions

Follow instructions for Lei Pattern #1 on p. 33.

Row 1. Olive ⅛" ribbon with Olive mustache.
Row 2 . Red mustache with Flame (fizz) whiskers.
Row 3. Yellow mustache with Sherbet (fizz) whiskers.

Purple Cigar

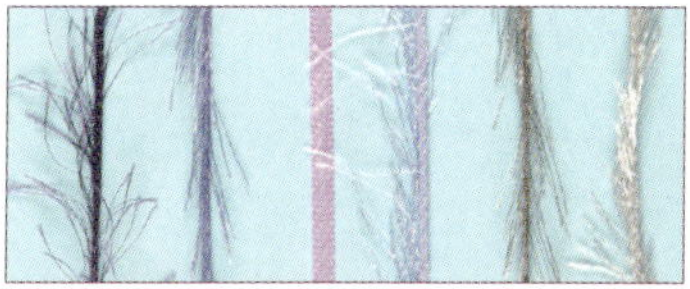

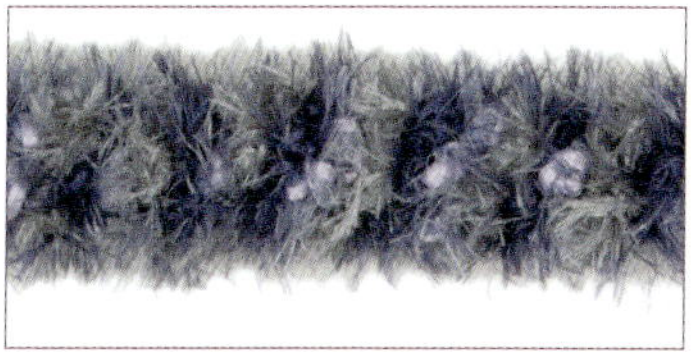

Supplies needed

- Dark Purple eyebrow
- Medium Purple eyebrow
- Lavender ⅛" ribbon
- Lavender eyebrow
- Gray eyebrow
- Gray mustache

Instructions

Follow instructions for Lei Pattern #1 on p. 33.

Row 1. Dark Purple eyebrow with Medium Purple eyebrow.

Row 2. Lavender ⅛" ribbon with Lavender eyebrow.

Row 3. Gray eyebrow with Gray mustache.

Marlene's Lei

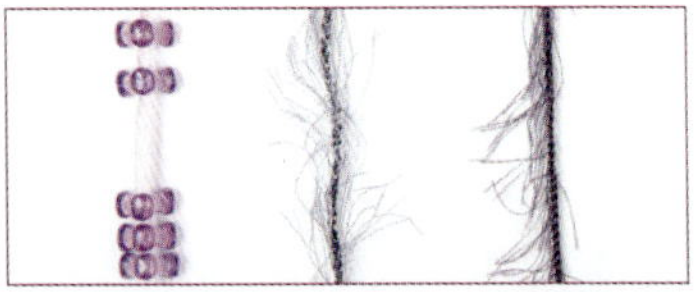

Supplies needed

- 200–300 Tri Beads
- Eyelash, two colors of your choice
- Crochet thread

Instructions

Follow instructions for Lei Pattern #6 on p. 44.

Row 1. Two colors of eyelash together.

Row 2. Beads on crochet thread.

Yellow Lehua with Pikake

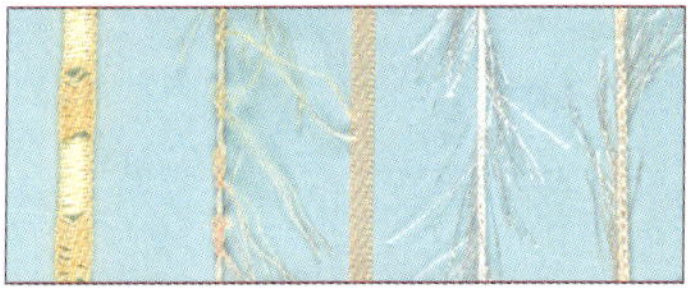

Supplies needed

- Yellow carisso
- Sherbet (fizz) whiskers
- Off-white ⅛" ribbon
- White eyebrow
- Off-white eyebrow

Instructions

Follow instructions for Lei Pattern #1 on p. 33.

Row 1. Yellow carisso with Sherbet (fizz) whiskers.
Row 2. Off-white ⅛" ribbon with White eyebrow.
Row 3. Off-white ⅛" ribbon with Off-white eyebrow.

Mixed Lei

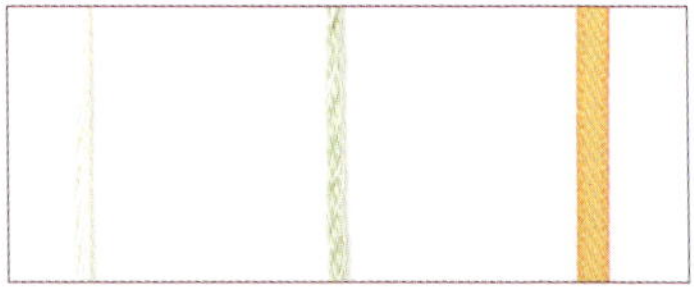

Supplies needed

- ⅛" Orange satin ribbon
- Green cotton twist
- Yellow mixed rattail

Instructions

Follow instructions for Lei Pattern #4 on p. 41.

1st lei: ⅛" Orange satin ribbon.
2nd lei: Green cotton twist.
3rd lei: Yellow mixed rattail.

Hat Lei with Fiori

Supplies needed

- Green mix boa
- Off-white Fiori
- Green eyebrow

Instructions

Follow instructions for Lei Pattern #7 on p. 45.

Row 1. Green mix boa with Green eyebrow.
Row 2. Off-white fiori, single crochet down the center of the lei.

Pikake

Supplies needed

- Off-white ⅛" satin ribbon

Instructions

Follow instructions for Lei Pattern #3 on p. 38.

Row 1. Use Off-white ⅛" satin ribbon.
Row 2. Use Off-white ⅛" satin ribbon.
Row 3. Use Off-white ⅛" satin ribbon.

Pearl Lei

Supplies needed

- 200–300 pearls
- Eskimo yarn, color of your choice
- Crochet thread

Instructions

Follow instructions for Lei Pattern #6 on p. 44.

Row 1. Two strands of Eskimo yarn together.

Row 2. Pearls on crochet thread.

Rosettes with Rattail

Supplies needed

- Multicolor rattail
- Green Erdal
- Green mixed fizz

Instructions

Follow instructions for Lei Pattern #3 on p. 38.

Row 1. Green Erdal with Green mix fizz.
Row 2. Mixed rattail.

Note: This lei has only 2 rows.

Straw Lei

Making Straw Lei

You can make yarn lei using one, two, three, four, and even five straws or pvc pipes which can be purchased at craft stores. You can even use chopsticks.

Making yarn lei with straws is a variation of crocheting. After all, crocheting is making knots and that's what you do with these straws. This is the easiest and fastest way to make a lei. Anyone can make these beautiful lei. The process is similar to the Hawaiian lei making method of wili, which is like a wrapping, twisting pattern.

Supplies needed

- Straws, pvc pipes, or chopsticks
- $\frac{5}{8}$" satin or grosgrain ribbon
- Yarn of your choice
- Scotch tape
- Scissors

Note: Eskimo yarn makes the lei look like a satin lei.

1-Straw

Supplies needed

- 1 straw
- 1 ball of yarn of your choice
- ⅝" satin ribbon
- Scotch tape
- Clothespin
- Small comb
- 2 kukui nuts

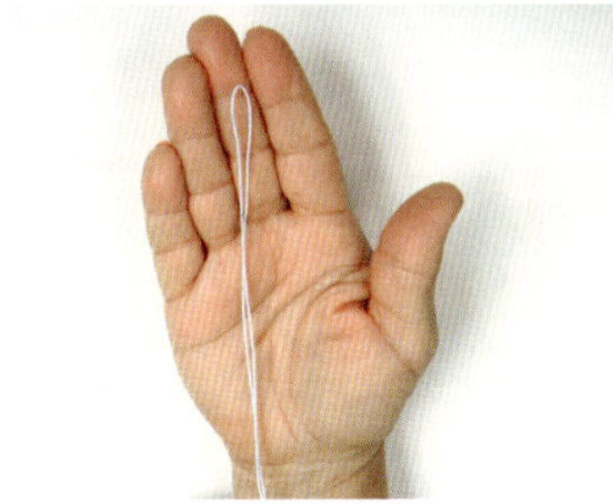

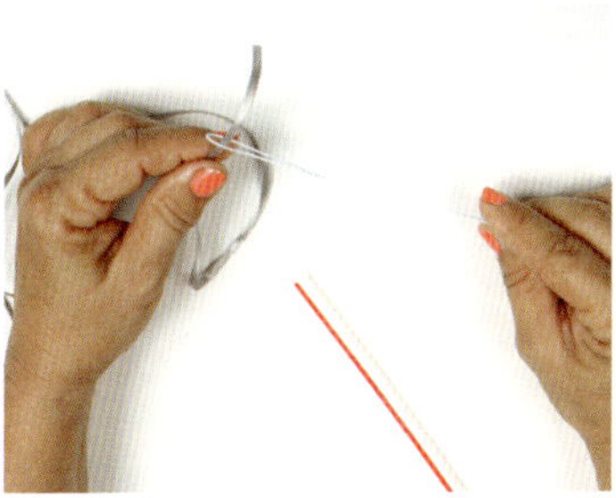

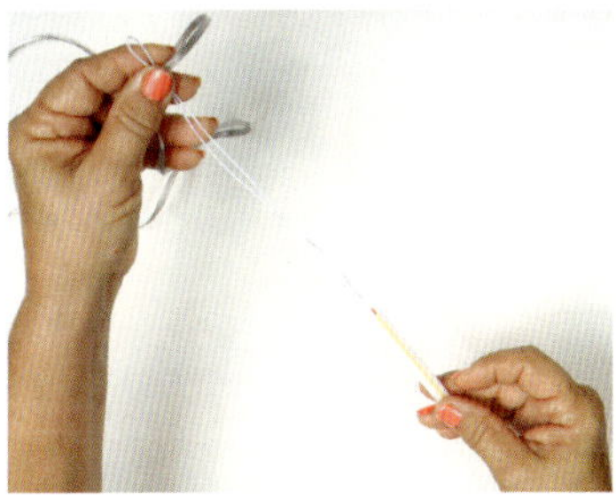

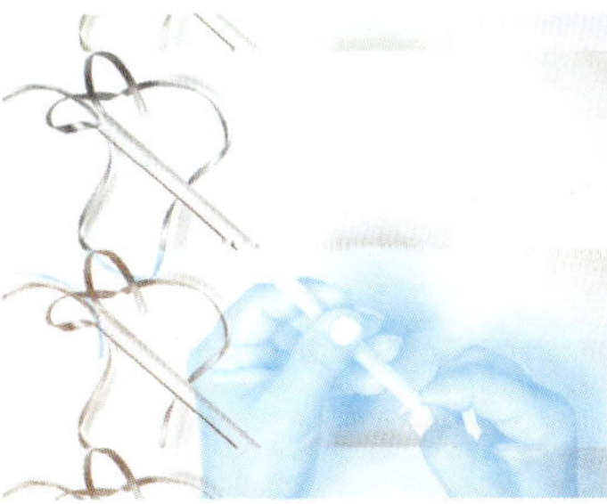

1. Take the ⅝" satin ribbon and push it through the straw (you can use a string to pull it through, a bobby pin, or wire to push it through).

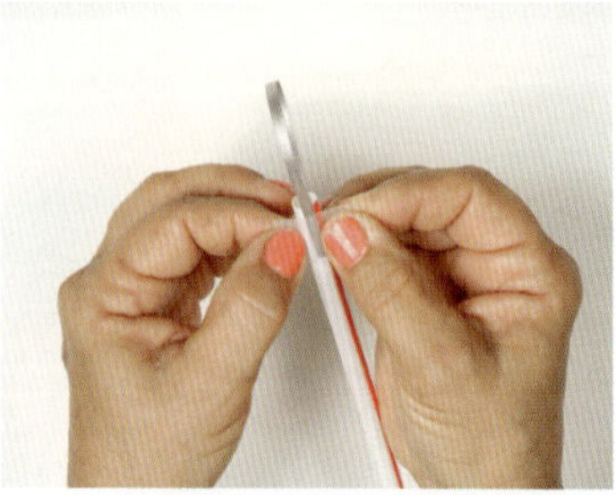

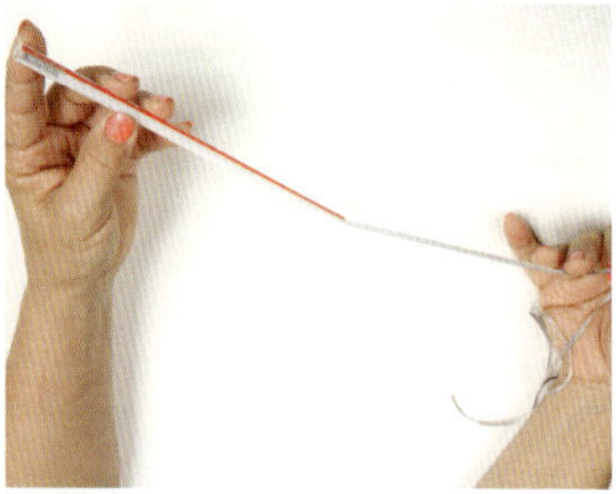

2. Take about an inch of the ribbon and tape it to the straw.

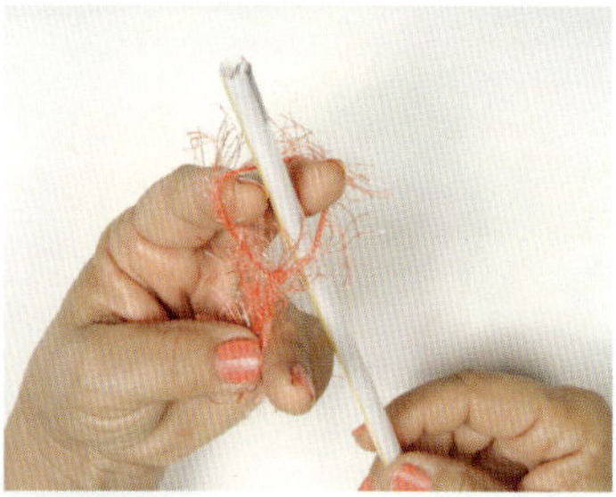

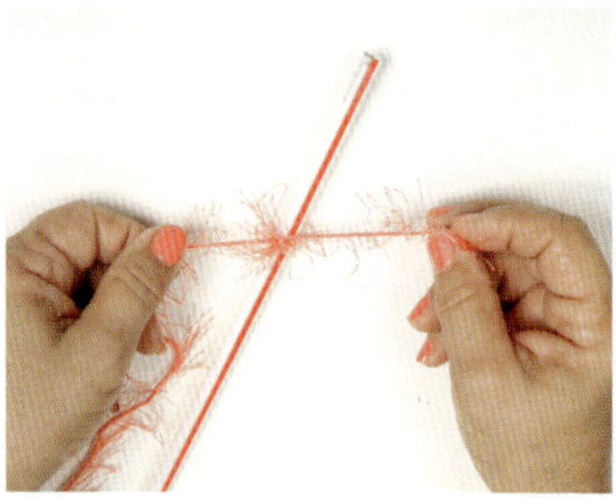

3. Tie end of yarn to straw.

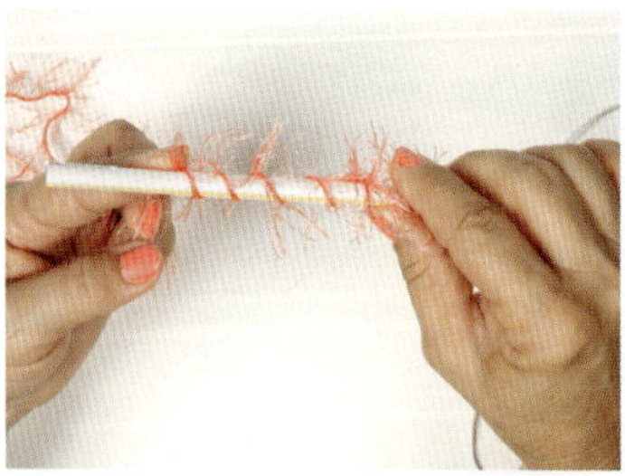

4. Wrap yarn around straw loosely.

5. When straw is filled, stop and comb yarns on straw to make it fluffy.

6. Push yarn down straw onto the ribbon (be sure you don't push it off the ribbon completely).

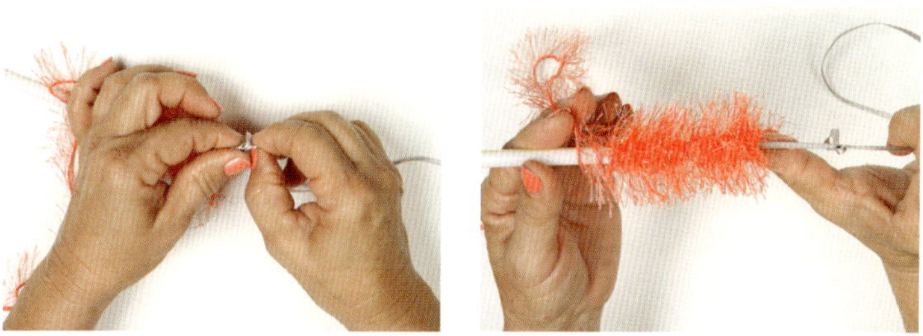

7. Use a clothespin at the end of the straw and keep pushing down until lei is finished. This is to make sure the yarn doesn't fall off the other end of the ribbon. Also, tie a knot at the end of the ribbon for security.

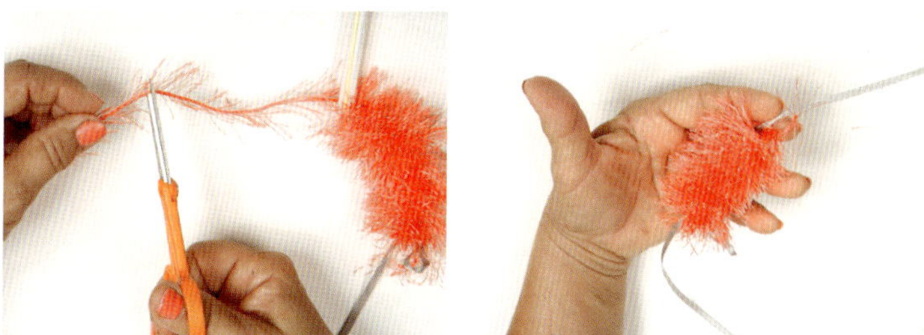

8. When you have used most of the yarn, leave enough so you can tie off the yarn on the straw before pushing down to the end. See Securing Your Lei on p. 48 to complete the lei.

2-Straw (Round)

Supplies needed

- 2 straws
- Yarn of your choice
- ⅛" satin ribbon, approx. 1¾ yards
- Scotch tape
- Small comb
- 2 kukui nuts

Note: Satin cord is used in photographic instructions so steps can be seen easily.

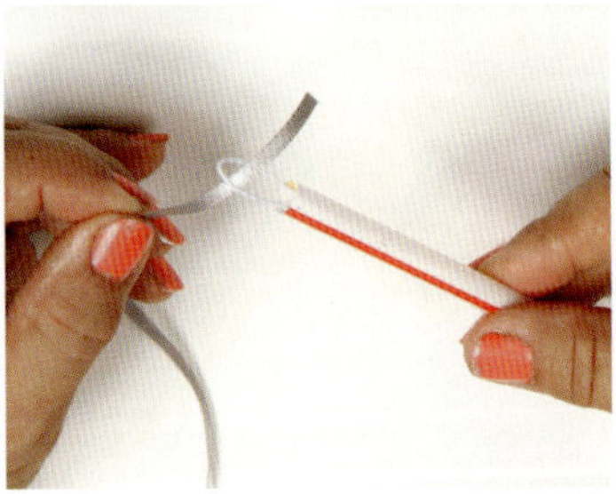

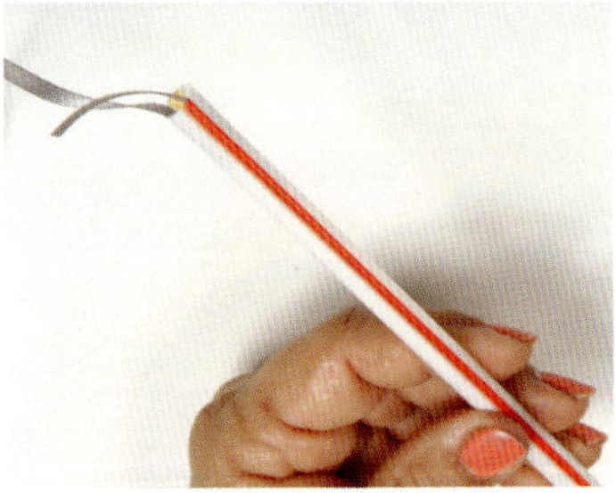

1. Take ⅛" satin ribbon and push through each straw.

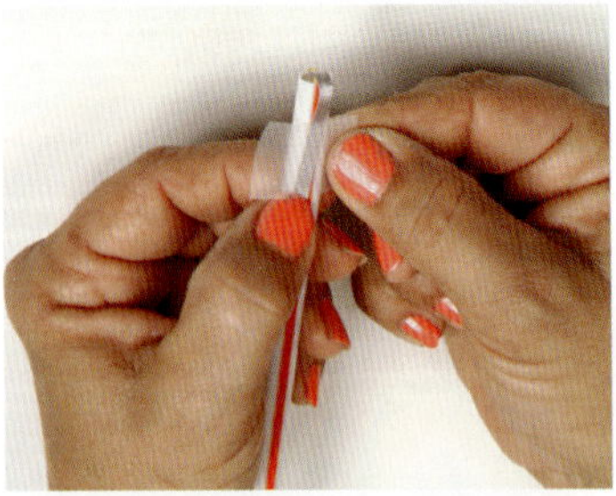

2. Secure end of satin ribbon to end of each straw with tape.

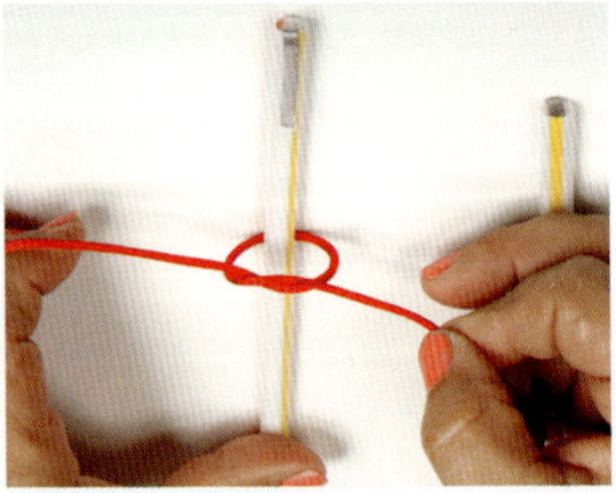

3. Tie yarn to one straw.

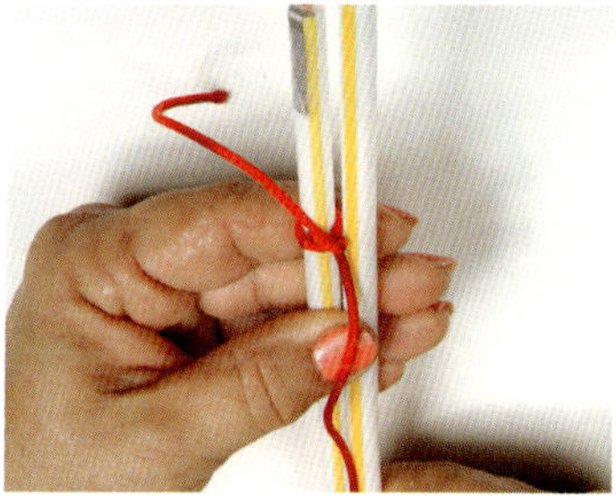

4. Hold the two straws together.

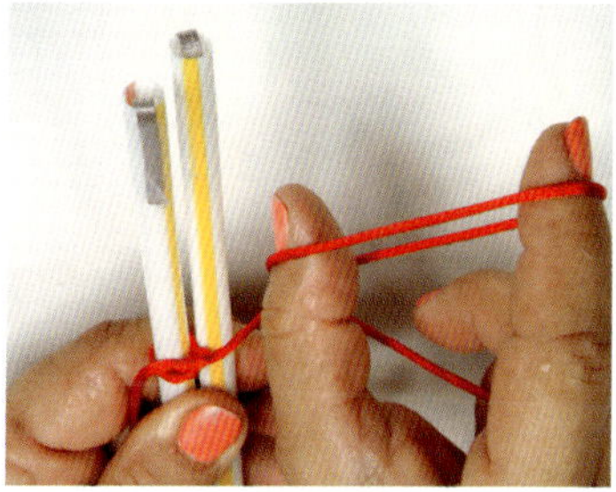

5. Wrap yarn around fingers.

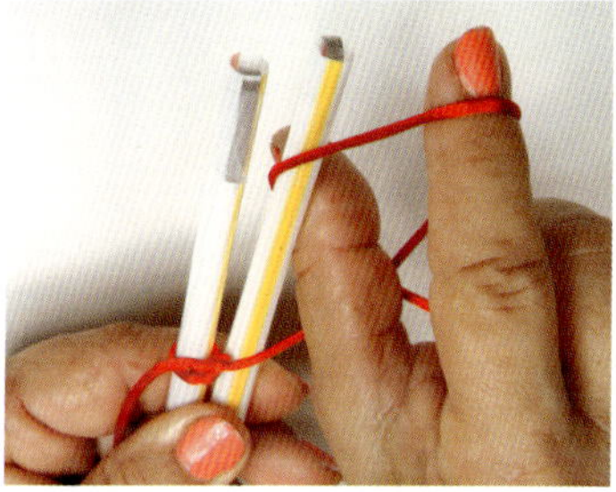

6. Turn and place on straw.

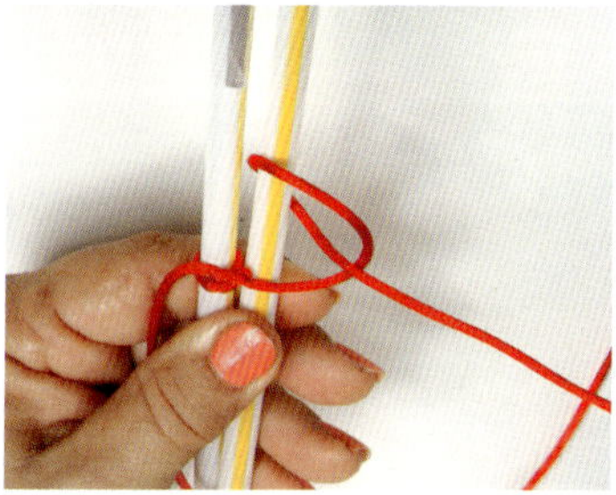

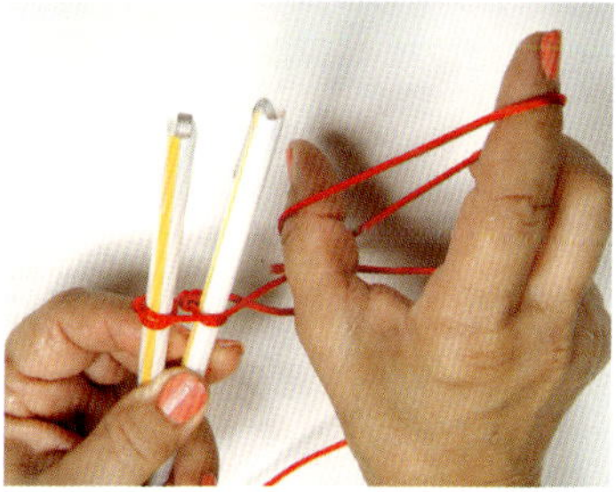

7. Turn counterclockwise and repeat on next straw.

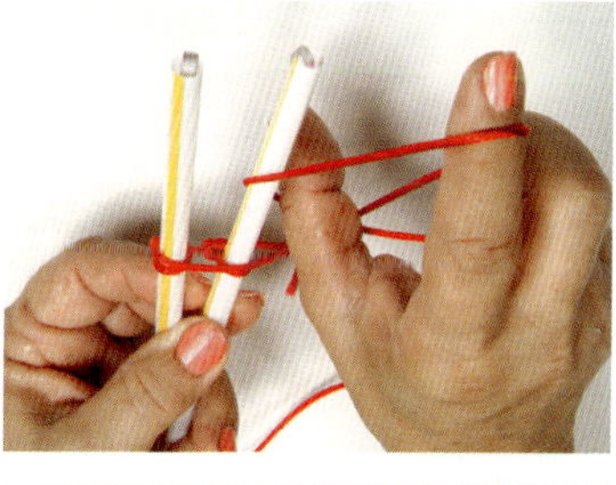

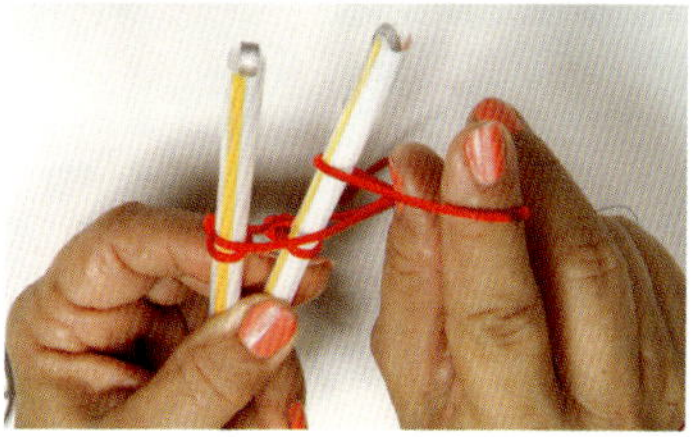

7. Continue until desired length. Tie both ribbons together.

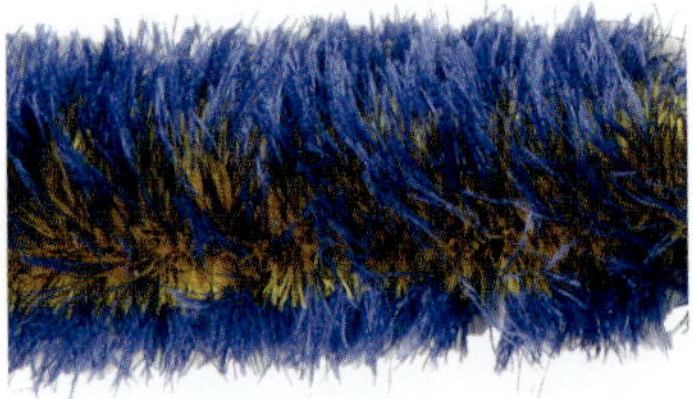

8. See Securing Your Lei on p. 48 to complete the lei.

2-Straw (Flat)

Supplies needed

- 2 straws
- Yarn of your choice
- ⅛" satin ribbon, approx. 1¾ yards
- Scotch tape
- Small comb
- 2 kukui nuts

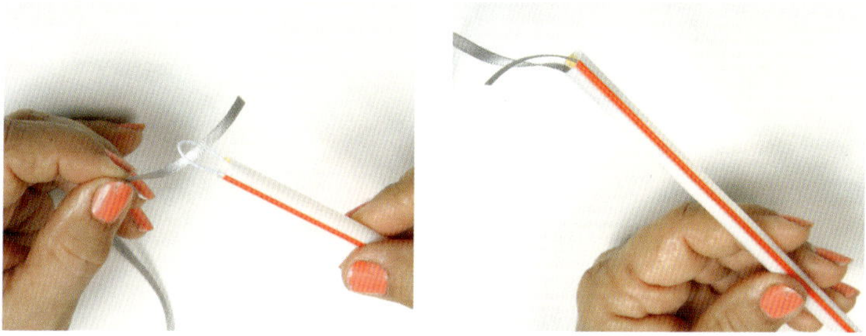

1. Take ⅛" satin ribbon and push through end of each straw.

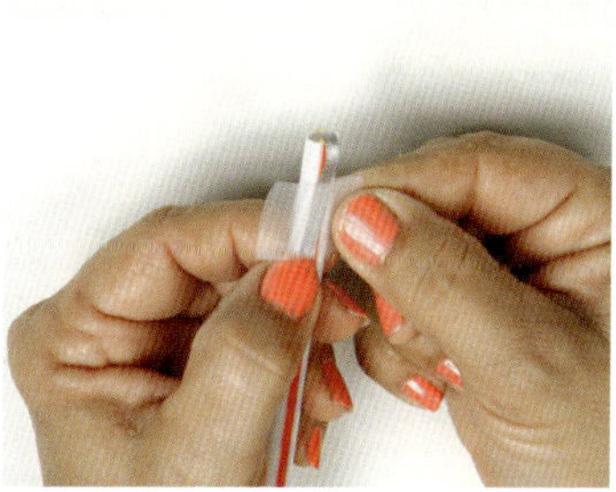

2. Secure end of satin ribbon to each straw with tape.

3. Tie yarn to one straw.

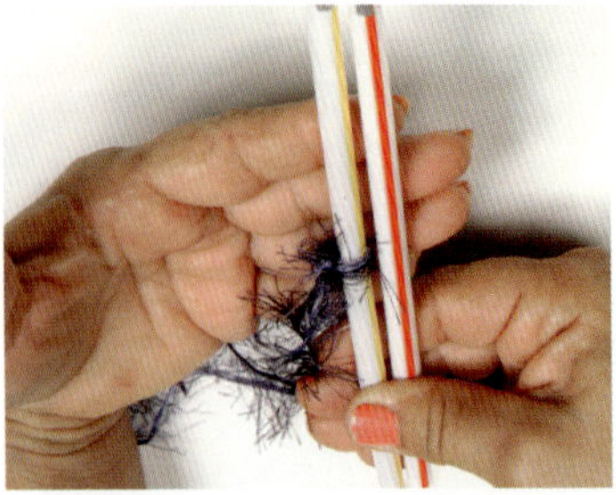

4. Hold both straws together.

5. Wrap around straws with a figure eight—loosely.

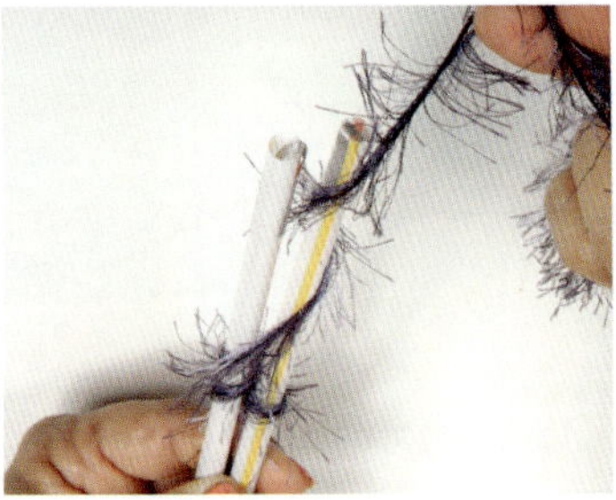

6. Turn counterclockwise and repeat on next straw.

7. When straw is full, use comb to fluff yarn.

8. Push down on to lead line.

9. Continue until desired length, (approx. 31" for neck lei).

10. See Securing Your Lei on p. 48 to complete the lei.

3-Straw

Supplies needed

- ⅛" satin ribbon, approx. 1¾ yards
- Yarn of your choice
- 3 straws
- Scotch tape
- 2 kukui nuts

Note: Satin cord is used in photographic instructions so steps can be seen easily.

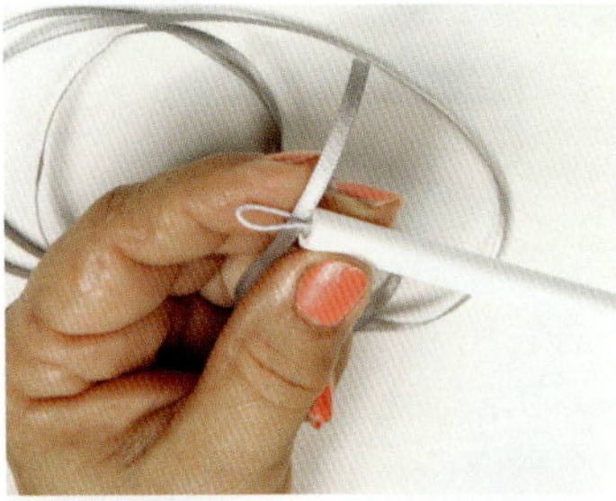

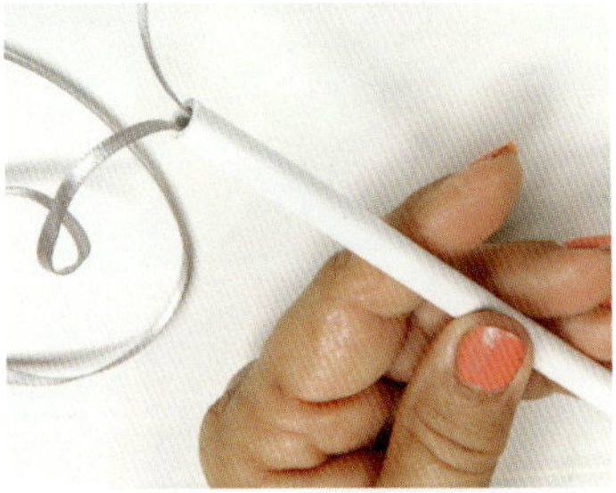

1. Take ⅛" ribbon and push through each straw.

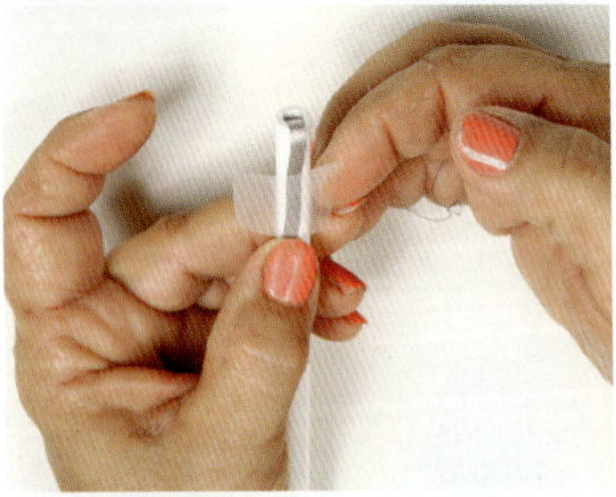

2. Secure end of ribbon to end of each straw with tape.

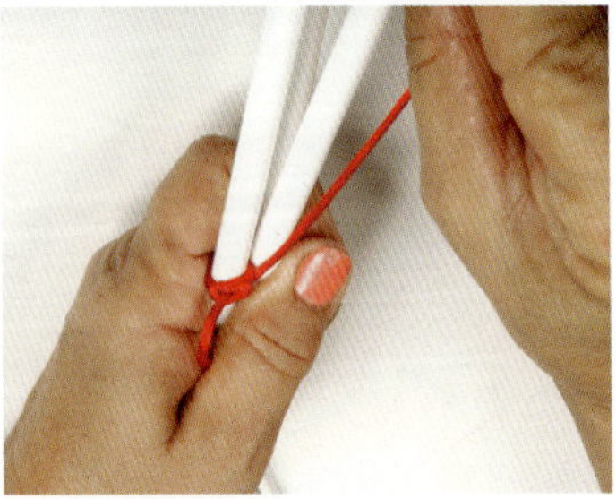

3. Tie yarn to one straw.

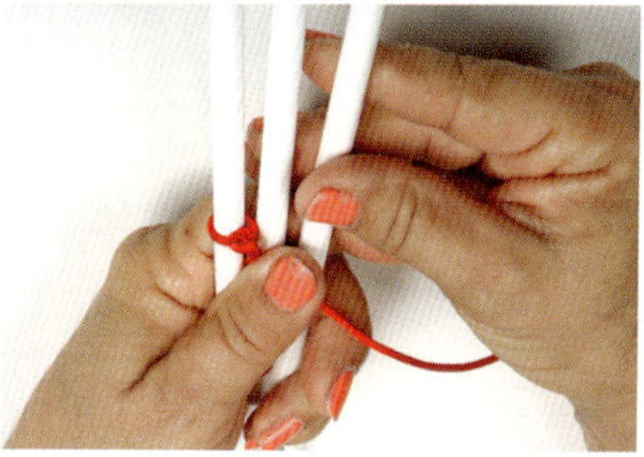

4. Hold three straws together.

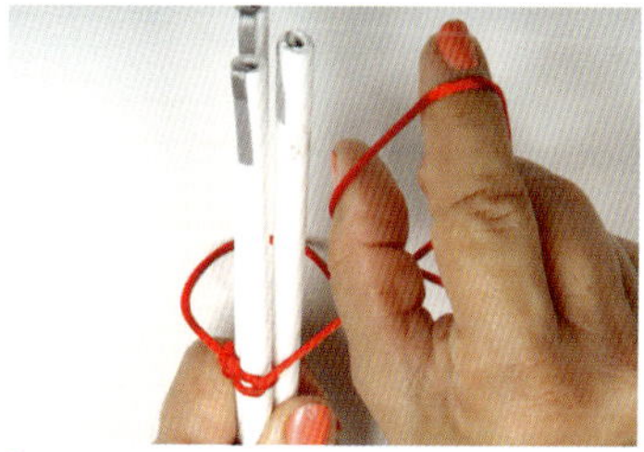

5. Wrap yarn around your fingers.

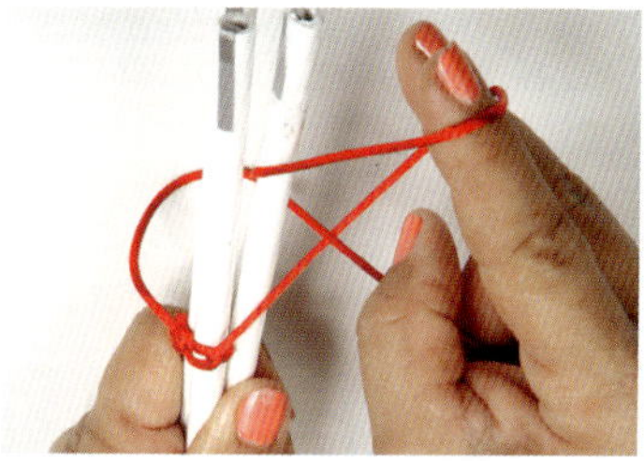

6. Turn and place on straw.

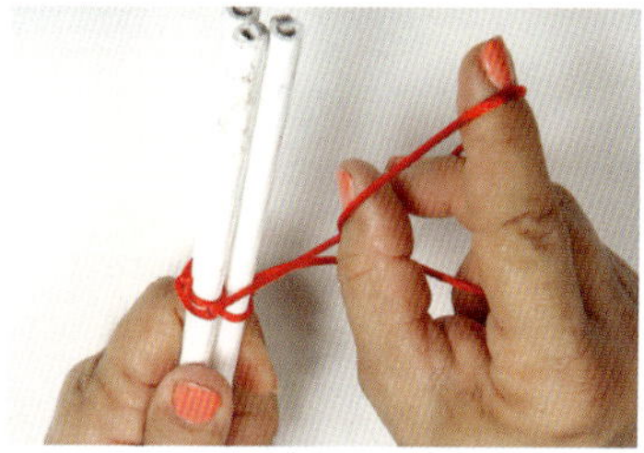

7. Turn counterclockwise and repeat on next straw.

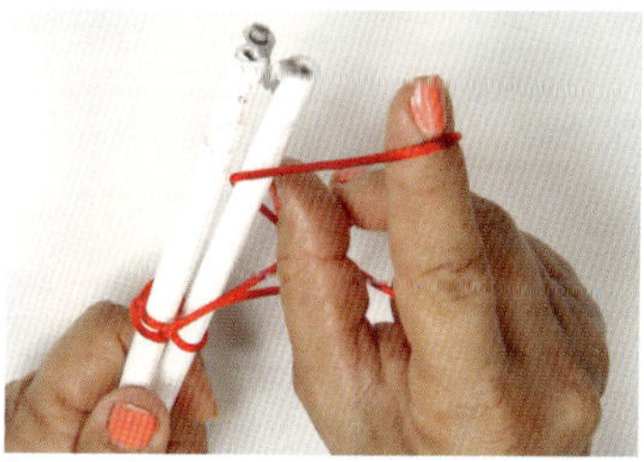

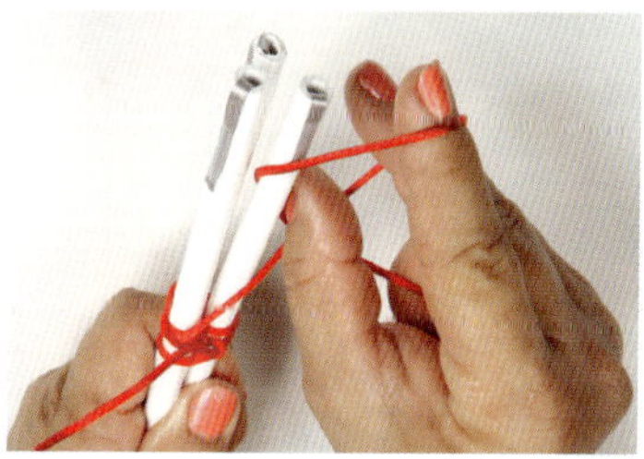

8. Continue until desired length. Tie all ribbons together.

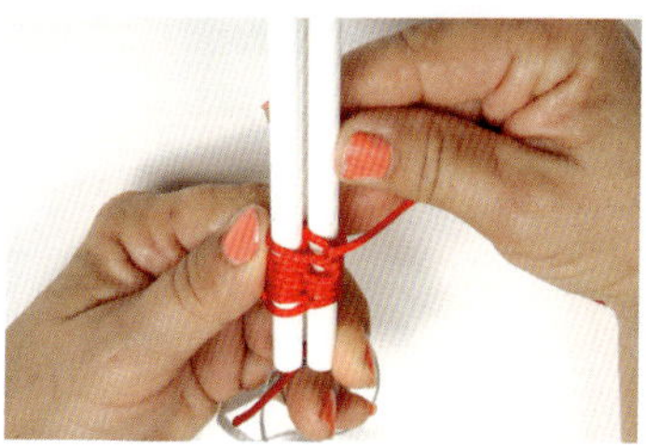

9. See Securing Your Lei on p. 48 to complete the lei.

4-Straw

Supplies needed

- ⅛" satin ribbon, approx. 1¾ yards
- Yarn of your choice
- 4 straws
- Scotch tape
- Small comb
- 2 kukui nuts

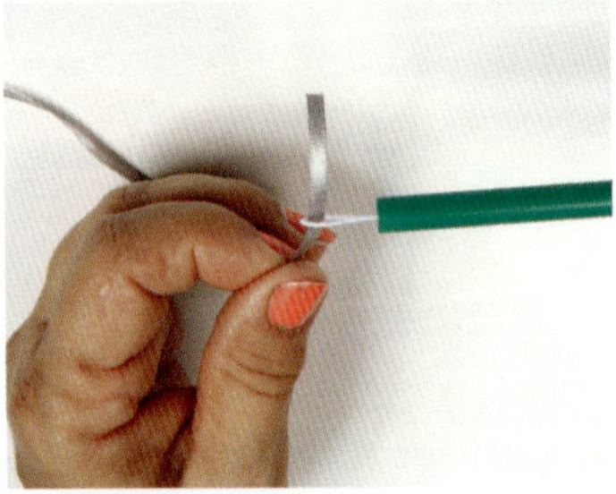

1. Take ⅛" ribbon and push through each straw. Secure end of ribbon to end of straw with tape.

2. Tie yarn to one straw.

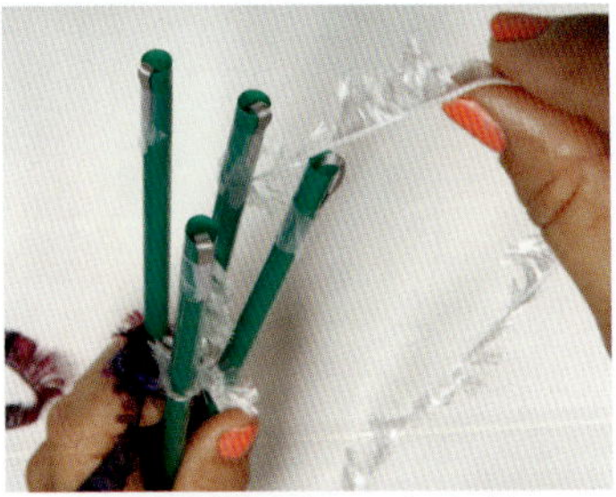

3. Hold the four straws together.

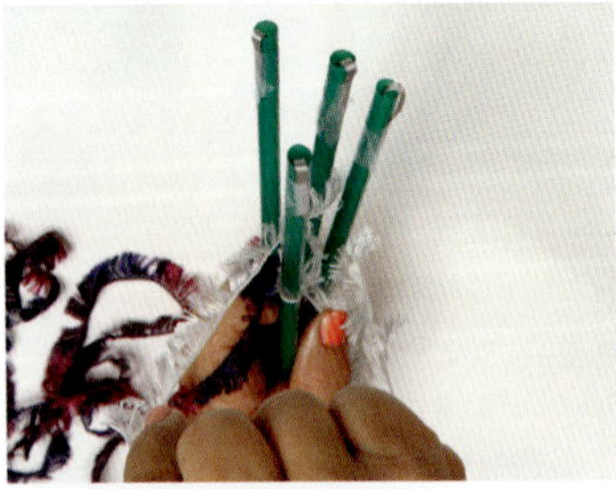

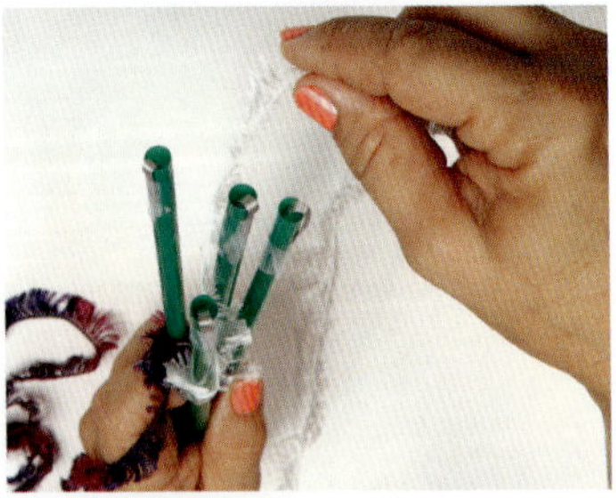

4. Wrap yarn around first straw counterclockwise, then clockwise around next straw.

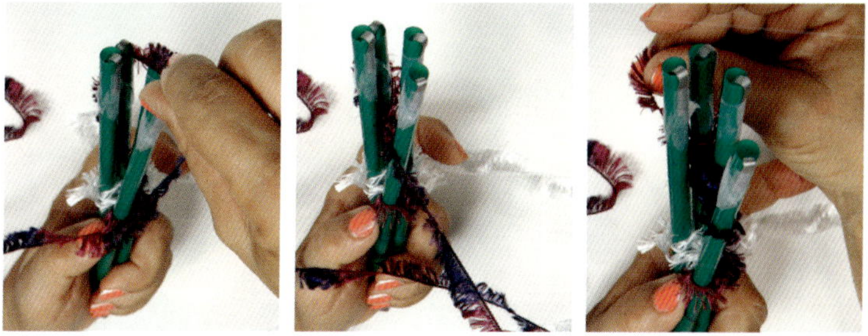

5. Repeat step 4, alternating straws.

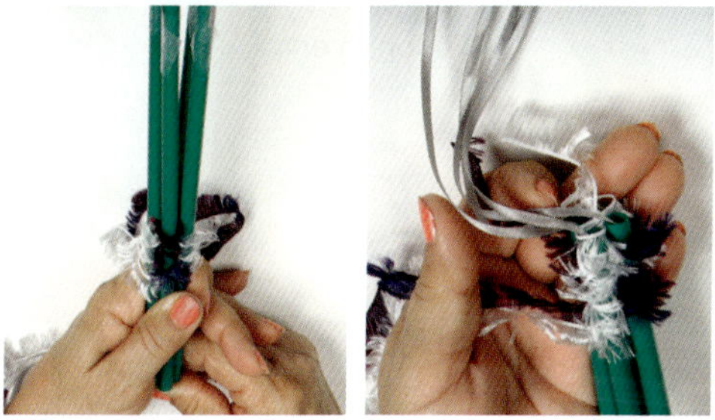

6. Push down yarn as you go, but be sure to leave some yarn on straw until lei is finished to desired length.

7. Remove ribbon from straws. Tie all four ribbons together.

8. See Securing Your Lei on p. 48 to complete the lei.

Rickrack Lei

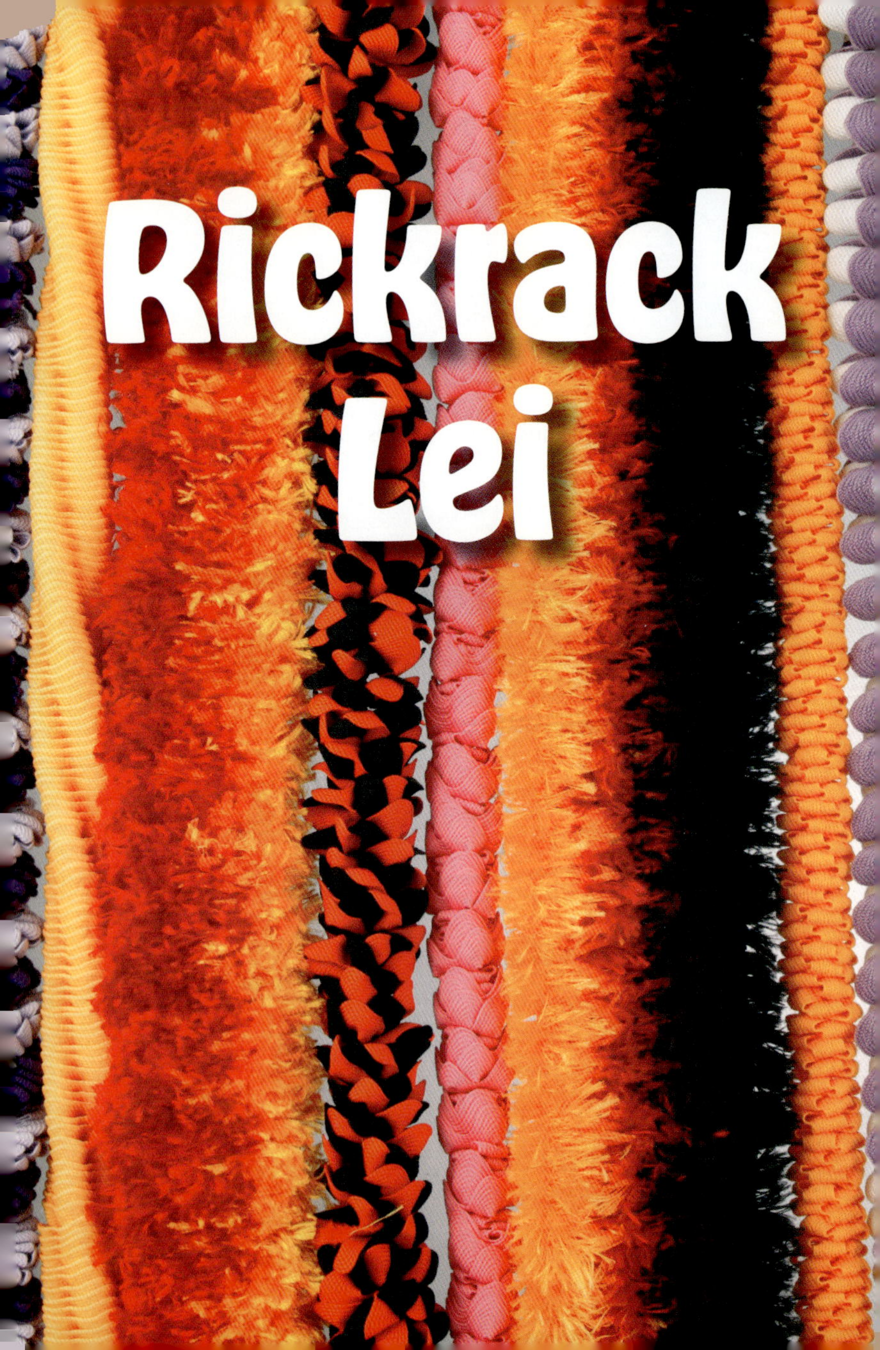

Making Rickrack Lei

Rickrack is a flat piece of trim in a zigzag shape historically used to finish the edges of fabric and to decorate clothing and curtains. Made from a variety of fibers including cotton, polyester, wool, and metallic fibers, it comes in many colors and is sturdy and washable.

In the 1970s, people in Hawai'i discovered how to make lei with rickrack. Using just a needle and thread, a wide variety of lei can be made that are extremely durable and washable. They make a lovely and lasting gift.

Try your hand at making some of these rickrack lei patterns that mimic flower lei like 'ilima, pīkake, and lokelani.

Instructions

Thread

1. Use 90" doubled on needle and knotted 3" from end.
2. Use button and carpet thread, silk twist button and buttonhold, bead stringing thread, or heavy-duty thread. (If 90" seems awkward, start with a shorter length of thread and add more later.)
3. Knot the bottom your thread leaving a 3" tail before starting to sew.

To Add More Thread

1. Leave enough thread for tying.
2. Re-thread needle with double thread and knot securely with remaining end. Leave knot snug against stitched rickrack.

To Add More Rickrack

1. Place new points over remaining points, leaving raw ends on inner fold of rickrack.
2. Continue stitching.

To End Lei

1. Cut remaining thread to 3".
2. Securely knot start and finish thread ends together. Rickrack ends

should meet snugly and knot should be hidden.

3. Tie a ribbon bow where the ends meet.

Length of Lei

Lei are usually 32 to 36" long. Yardage is given accordingly. Length will vary depending on whether or not you work loosely or tightly.

Hint: After making the first few inches, an easy rhythm of stitches and patterns develops.

Blossom Lei

Supplies needed

- 8 packages jumbo rickrack
- Button and carpet thread

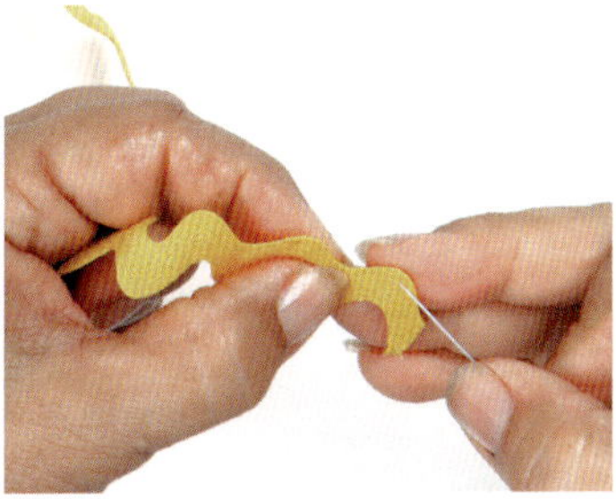

1. Stitch along one edge through each point, alternating direction of stitch from front to back.

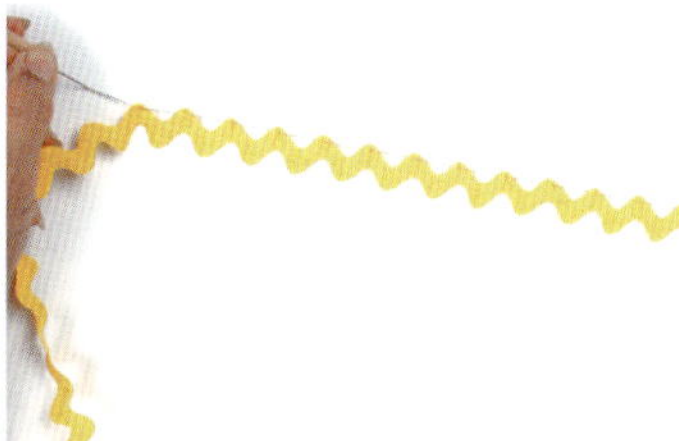

2. Gather rickrack into flowers every few inches, twisting in same direction each time.

3. See To End Lei on p. 83 to complete the lei.

Golden Spiral ʻIlima

Supplies needed

- 10 (2½ yard) packages Gold rickrack, medium
- Needle and thread

1. Stitch down through tip of each point, along one side only.

2. Overlap 4 points to form a star with points curving downwards.

3. Repeat steps, fitting each star on top of one before. The lei will twist itself when finished.

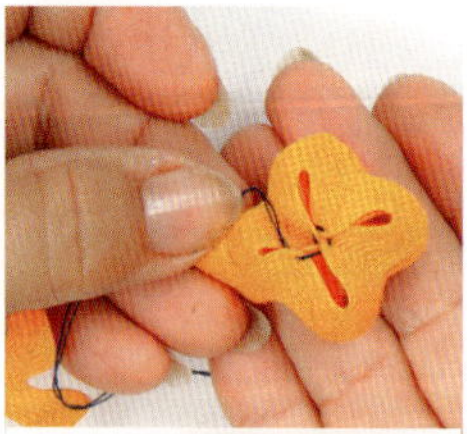

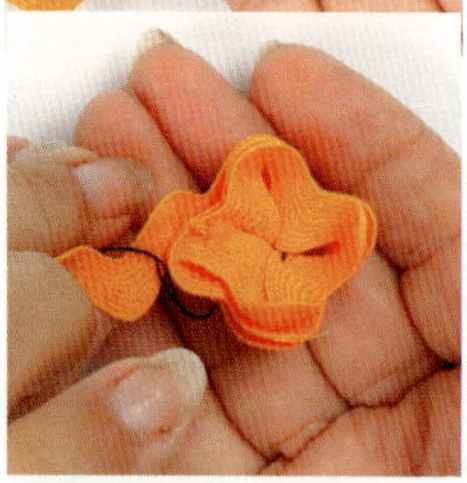

4. Repeat until you reach the desired length.

5. See To End Lei on p. 83 to complete the lei.

Lilac

Supplies needed

- 12 yards Lavender rickrack
- 12 yards Purple rickrack

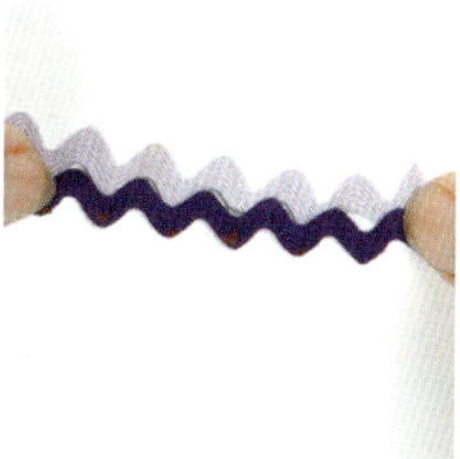

1. Keep one color rickrack to left. Keep one color to right with points overlapping slightly at start.

2. Stitch in one set of overlapping points, then stitch out the next set. Keep the position of your colors and overlap consistent.

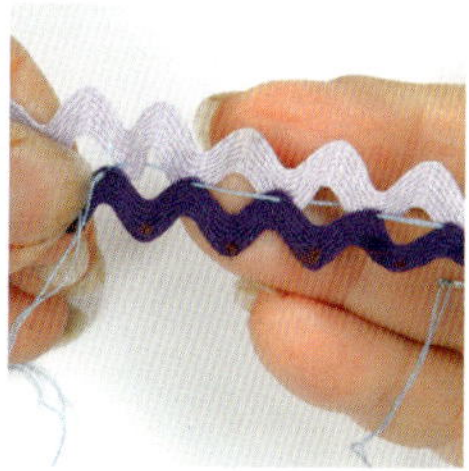

3. After several groups of stitches, slide rickrack toward knotted end of thread, twisting it in one direction.

4. See To End Lei on p. 83 to complete the lei.

Pikake

Supplies needed

- 21 yards White rickrack

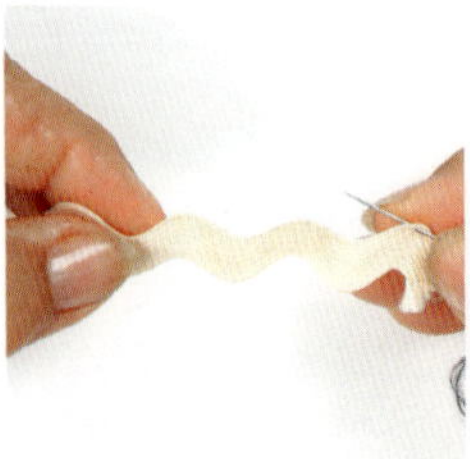

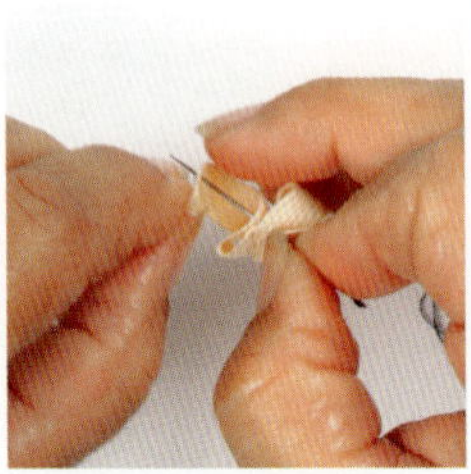

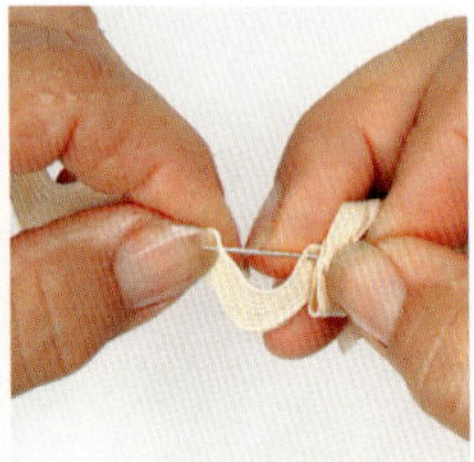

1. Insert needle into top point and push out through lower point. Repeat for eleven points. Gather tightly to form flower center (2 units).

2. Stitch up through thirteen points along upper edge. Pull gently on thread, twisting rickrack over center to form petals. Arrange into three units resting in each other, with petals alternating. Push firmly to hold section in blossom.

3. Repeat steps 1 and 2 to end.

4. See To End Lei on p. 83 to complete the lei.

Lokelani

To make a Lokelani lei, use Pink rickrack and follow the steps for Pīkake.

Plumeria

Supplies needed

- 4 packages medium-size rickrack (approx. 10 yards)
- 3 packages jumbo rickrack in contrasting colors (approx. 7½ yards)
- 5 dozen small colored beads

1. Beginning with jumbo rickrack, stitch through every third point, alternating direction of stitch from front to back. Gather rickrack after seventh stitch.

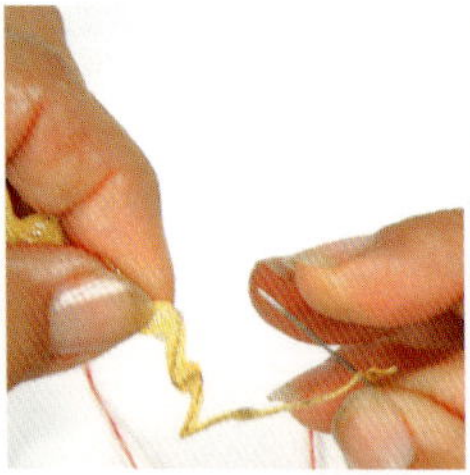

2. Continue with medium rickrack, stitching in same manner, but cut rickrack after seventh stitch. Add bead and gather.

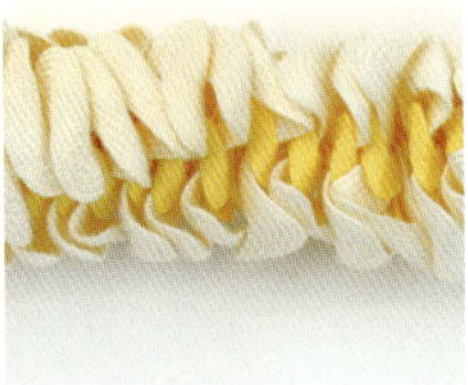

3. Repeat steps 1 and 2.

4. See To End Lei on p. 83 to complete the lei.

Mauna Loa

Supplies needed

- 2 colors jumbo rickrack (4 packages each)
- Button and carpet thread

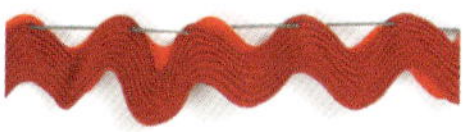

1. Place one color rickrack evenly over second color. Treat this combination as one.

2. Stitch through the first and third points from front and back.

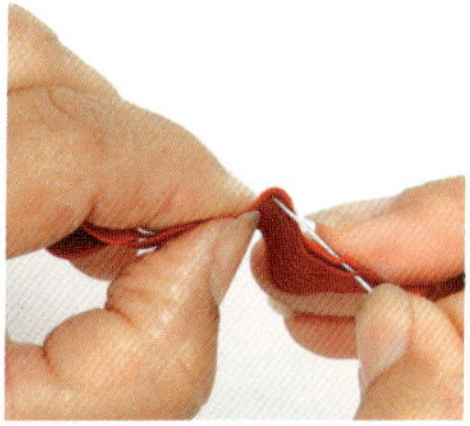

3. Stitch through the fourth and sixth points from back to front. Adjust each point to fit over preceding one.

4. See To End Lei on p. 83 to complete the lei.

Money Lei

Making Money Lei

A money lei is always appreciated, cherished, and loved. It is arguably the best and most memorable lei compared to any floral lei. The best thing is that a money lei has value after it is worn. It has life after the occasion—spending life!

A money lei is given on birthdays using the dollar amount of the person's age. It is often given at retirement parties using the amount of years in dollars. But most of all, a money lei is very popular in Hawai'i during graduation season using school colors.

A money lei is a monetary gift and a lei of love that can be made with bills and/or coins. These lei combine the Japanese art of origami and tradition of monetary gift-giving with the Hawaiian art of lei making. Dollar bills folded origami-style and made into a lei puts a contemporary, cultural twist on the traditional lei. For best folding results, use a new, crisp bill. Line up all edges and corners as precisely as possible. Fold on a hard, flat surface. Good lighting is a must. If you cannot get new bills, iron clean, nice bills to smooth and remove the wrinkles and moisture of used bills. Use medium heat. You can also add purchased embellishments such as stickers, confetti, pre-made laser-cut designs, large paper punch-outs, and clip art found online.

All U.S. currency is government property. It is legal to fold and tape bills, but illegal to intentionally destroy money by gluing, cutting, or tearing it in any manner. Use the least amount of tape as possible. When taking apart a money lei, SLOWLY and GENTLY remove the double-sided tape. Rub off the tape to prevent damage to the bill.

Graduation Cap Dollar Lei

Makes a 72" lei.

One bill makes one cap. Assorted colors of mini tassels may also be purchased by the yard as tassel trim. Trim the sharp tips of the Mylar graduation caps to smooth the edges. Hot glue is best to secure the diplomas to the ribbon.

Materials

- 10 dollar bills, crisp
- 2 yards ribbon, acetate, #9, (1½"), blue
- 2 yards ribbon, acetate, #5, (⅞"), white w/ blue graduation print
- 6 yards tape, double-sided tape, 3⁄16"
- 2 yards tape, single-sided, ¾"
- 10 mini tassels, black (1 pack)
- 1 cardboard, thin, 2 x 10"
- 10 "diploma" computer printouts on copy paper
- 10 confetti scrapbook cutouts, large Mylar graduation caps, blue
- 10 sequins, 8 mm, black
- 1 hot glue gun and 3 glue sticks
- 1 tape measure
- 1 scissors

1. Cut a 2 x 2" square piece of cardboard. Crease along three borders of the bill. Slide the cardboard through the creased border.

2. Tape the edges of the bill to the cardboard using single-sided tape. Blue tape is used for this photo.

3. Fold the bill around the cardboard. Fold in the end of the bill. Tape the bill around the cardboard using double-sided tape. Show the eagle on the top of the cap.

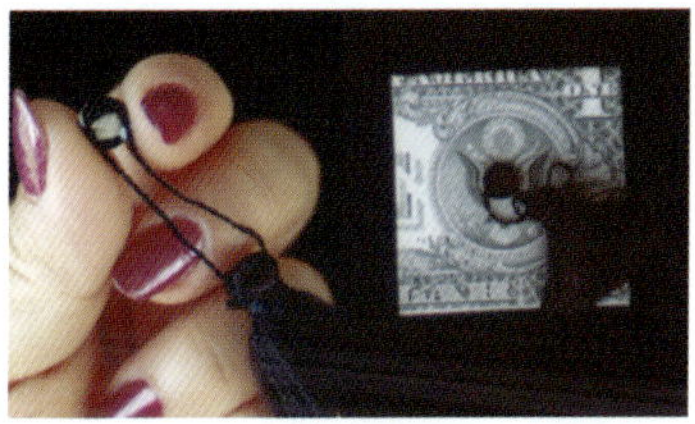

4. Make a small ball using double-sided tape. Stick the tassel cord under the sequin. Stick the sequin onto the middle of the folded bill. Repeat steps 1 to 4 for nine additional bills.

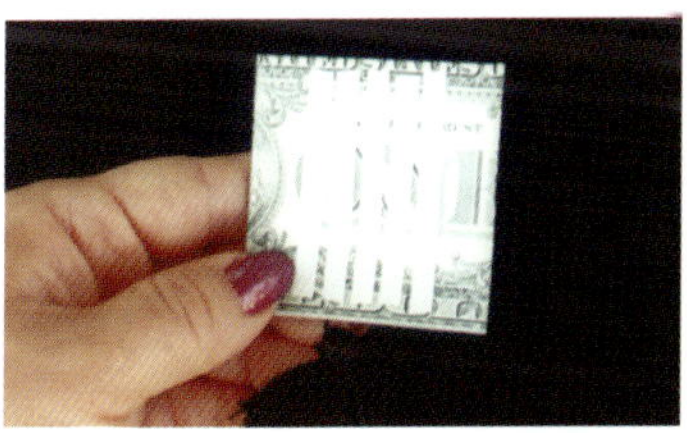

5. Place a lot of double-sided tape along the back of the dollar cap.

6. Print, cut, roll, and tape ten diploma signs from your computer.

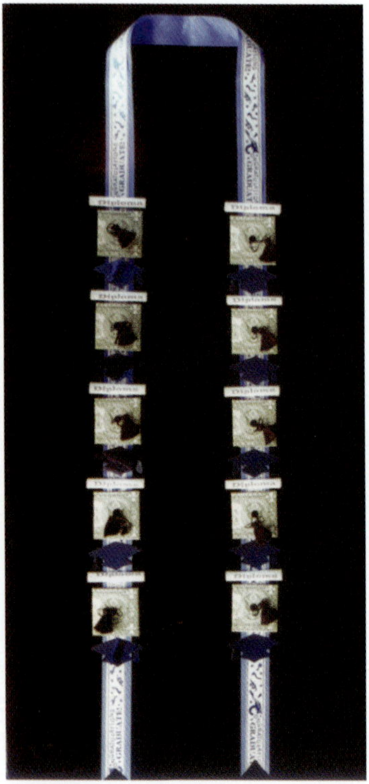

7. Cut a strip of #9 blue ribbon 72" in length. Cut a strip of #5 graduation ribbon 72" in length. Place a long strip of double-sided tape on the back of the graduation ribbon. Peel off the paper backing of the tape. Stick on the graduation ribbon to the front center of the blue ribbon. Cut the two ends of the ribbon to a "w" tip. Place and tape the dollar caps, diplomas, and confetti onto the ribbon, spaced evenly. Start 5" from the ends of the ribbon.

Long Dollar Graduation Lei

Makes a 68" lei.

May use computer printout on cardstock paper to substitute for centerpiece fountain trim. Working on the floor is best. Tape the long dollar and ribbons to the floor to hold them steady.

Materials

- 10 dollar bills, crisp
- 6 yards tape, double-sided 3/16"
- 1 graduation centerpiece cascade fountain or similar for 18 to 20 decoration cutouts
- 8' ribbon, acetate, #3 (5/8"), yellow
- 8' ribbon, acetate, #3 (5/8"), purple
- 2 graduation plush toys or similar
- 1 tape measure
- 1 scissors

1. Place double-sided tape along the right edge of the bill. Continue this step for a total of nine bills. The last bill will not need taping.

2. Peel off the paper backing of the tape. Stick another bill to the taped edge to join the bills. Continue until all bills are joined.

3. Cut a strip of yellow ribbon 80" in length. Cut a strip of purple ribbon 80" in length. Add the double-sided tape to the back center of each strip of ribbon. Start and end the tape about 10" from the ends of the ribbon. Keep the ribbon ends free for streamers. Tape the two ribbon strips along the center of the long, joined bill, leaving 10" of ribbon on each end for the streamers.

4. Tape on the decorative hats and trim to the long, joined bills spaced evenly using double-sided tape. Bend the lei in half. Tape the second half of the trim in the opposite direction.

5. Tie the yellow and purple streamers into a knot at the ends of the bill strip.

6. Tear the yellow and purple 18" ribbons in half to create two thinner ribbon strips. Insert the ribbon strips into the streamer knots.

7. Add in the plush toy. Tie a knot in front of the toy. Curl the ends of the thin ribbon. Repeat steps 5 to 7 for the other end of the lei. Trim the streamers evenly.

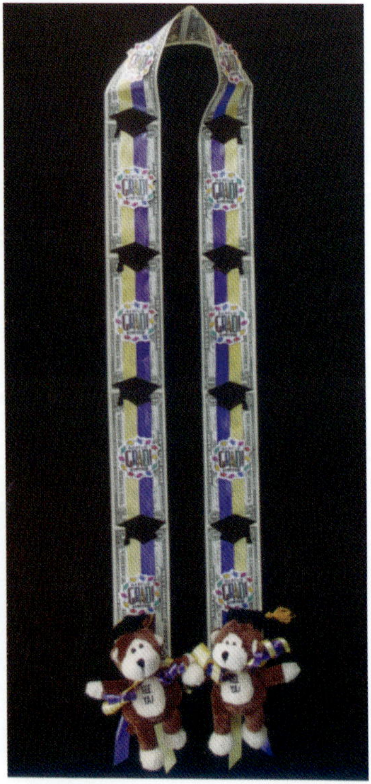

Daisy Dollar Lei

Makes a 70" lei.

Three bills make one daisy. For a greenish flower, use the back of the dollar bill. Place glue in the hole where you cut the stem off the silk flower using the tip of a wire. Glue helps to keep the flower petal layers together.

Materials

- 24 dollar bills, crisp
- 1 stem silk daisy flowers, or similar, yellow (8 blooms)
- 2 yards ribbon, acetate, #9 (1½"), white
- 2 yards ribbon, acetate, #5 (⅞"), yellow
- 3 yards tape, double-sided, 3/16"
- 12 butterflies, nylon, 1", yellow
- 4 florist wires, #26 or similar
- 3 yards thread, carpet/button, white
- 1 sewing needle
- 1 hot glue gun and 3 glue sticks
- 1 wire cutter
- 1 pen
- 1 tape measure
- 1 scissors

1. Fold the bill in half widthwise to form a crease. Open the bill.

2. Fold the two sides of the bill inward toward the center crease.

3. Fold the bill in half lengthwise.

4. Fold the four corners of the bill inward to the center crease.

5. Fold the top and bottom sides of the bill inward to the center crease.

6. Fold the bill into fourths lengthwise in an accordion-pleated pattern. Repeat steps 1 to 6 for two additional bills.

7. Fold the three bills in half widthwise to form a crease. Place the two bills on the outside facing the same direction.

8. Cut a piece of wire into thirds. Tie the wire around the center of the three folded bills. Place the center bill facing the opposite direction. Twist the wire tight, securing the three bills.

9. Open the petals using the back of a pen.

10. Cut off the excess wire using a wire cutter. Use the back of a pen to flatten down the wire against the flower. Tie a 10" thread around the wire. Leave the thread long. Add double-sided tape to the back of the flowers. Place the tape over the thread.

11. Cut pieces of white and yellow ribbon 70" in length. Tape the yellow ribbon to the center of the white ribbon using a 70" strip of double-sided tape. Cut the ends to a "w" tip. Position the four money flowers, four silk daisies, and five butterflies evenly on each side of the ribbon. Start 3" from the ends of the ribbon.

12. Peel off the paper backing of the tape. Stick and sew the money flowers to the ribbon using a sewing needle. Glue the silk daisies and butterflies onto the ribbon. Trim any loose threads.

Floweret Dollar Kukui Nut Lei

Makes a 40" lei.

One bill makes one floweret. May substitute button/carpet thread for rubber bands.

Materials

- 22 dollar bills, crisp
- 22 kukui nuts, black
- 44 cowry shell rings
- 22 rubber bands, small white
- 1½ yards tape, double-sided, 3/16"
- 1 sewing needle
- 3 yards thread, button/carpet, white
- 1 toothpick
- 1 scissors

1. Fold the bill widthwise into ⅛" folds, creating an accordion pattern.

2. Place a rubber band in the center of the bill to secure the folds. Wrap the rubber band twice over the bill if needed.

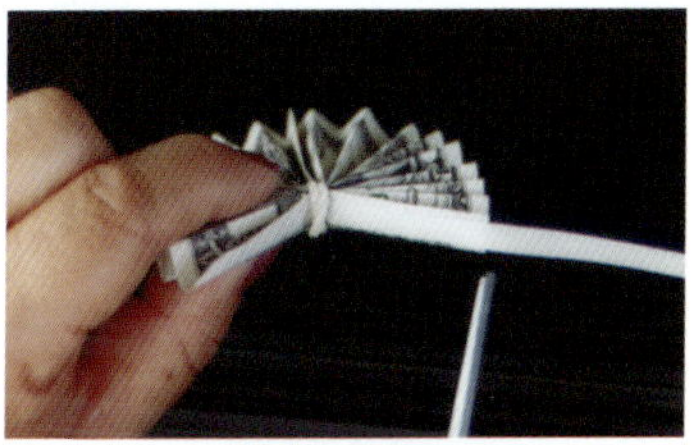

3. Place double-sided tape along the two sides of the folded bill. Peel off the paper backing.

4. Stick the ends of the bill together, forming a circle.

5. Cut a piece of thread 104" in length. Thread the needle. Fold the thread in half. Tie a knot 6" from the open end of the thread. Attach a toothpick to the knotted end to secure the first kukui nut. String through one kukui nut and one shell ringlet.

6. Insert the needle through the rubber band loop, then out through the space between the taped edges of the bill. Pull the bill down to the last shell ringlet.

7. String on one ringlet to secure the bill. Repeat steps 1 to 7 until lei is completed.

8. Tie a knot to join and secure the lei. Add a bow if desired.

Rose Dollar Lei

Makes a 40" lei.

Two bills make one rose. Substitute colored paper for bills to cut cost. Use them in the center of the rose.

Materials

- 72 dollar bills, crisp
- 1 roll tape, double-sided, 3/16"
- 1 roll transparent tape, ½"
- 36 poly calyx 1½ x 2"
- 3 yards thread, button craft, white
- 1 sewing needle, long
- 1 pen (covered)
- 1 tape measure
- 1 scissors

1. Fold the bill in half lengthwise to crease. Open the bill.

2. Fold the two sides of the bill inward to the crease.

3. Fold the bill in half lengthwise. Repeat steps 1 to 3 for a second bill.

4. Open up the last fold of the bills. Tape along the right edge of one of the folded bills using double-sided tape.

5. Stick the second bill onto the first bill along the taped edge. Place the bills facing the same direction.

6. Fold the attached bills in half lengthwise on the existing crease.

7. Hold 1" from one end of the bill strip. Fold the two sides of the end of the bill inward to create a tubular stem.

8. Hold the stem end of the bill. Bend the bill strip over your thumb to the left.

9. Wrap the bill backward around your thumb. Pinch the bill to hold it in place.

10. Make a backward and downward fold. Twist the stem in your left hand to the right while wrapping the bill strip in your right hand toward the left.

11. Make another backward and downward fold.

12. Twist the stem to the right while wrapping the dollar strip around creating the rose petals. Stop when you have twisted up to the end of the downward fold. Continue this step with the backward and downward fold while twisting the stem to the right. Continue this step until 1" from the end of the strip. Pinch the petals together to shape the rose.

13. Wrap the remaining end of the dollar strip around the stem. Keep the stem thin. Tape down the end of the bill by wrapping a piece of transparent tape around the stem to secure the rose for stringing.

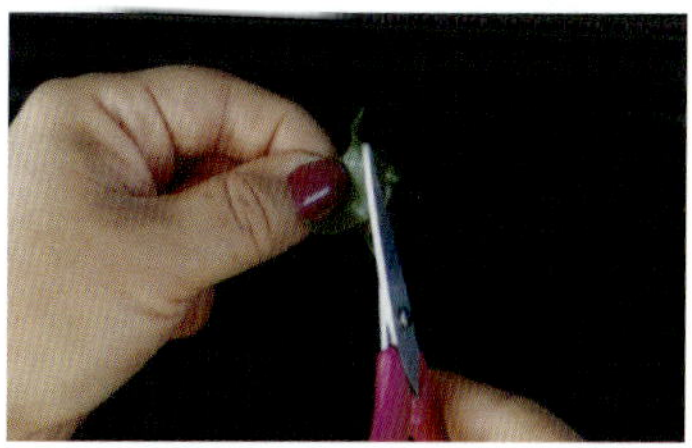

14. Cut off the base of the calyx to enlarge the opening.

15. Insert the rose stem into the calyx.

16. Open the rose using a closed pen.

17. Cut a strip of thread 104" in length. Fold the thread in half. Tie a knot 6" from the open end of the thread. Hook on a lei needle. If using a sewing needle, thread the needle before tying the knot. Pierce the roses onto the needle from the top of the flower through the stem. Do not pierce the bills. Pull the roses down to the thread knot. Insert the stems into the previously strung flowers to hide the taped ends.

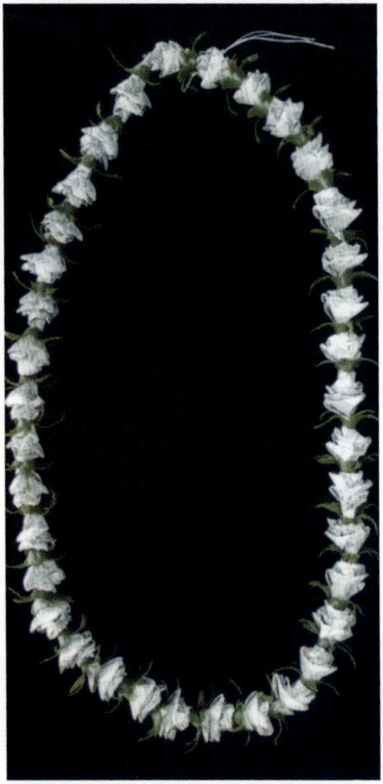

18. Continue until all roses are strung. Tie a knot to join the lei. Add a bow if desired.

Shell Lei

Making Shell Lei

Throughout Hawai'i's history, shells were used as food (live shells); tools such as files and chisels, lures, fishhooks, fishnet weights, trumpets, medicine; body and clothes adornments; toys; for ceremonial and religious purposes; and occasionally money.

'Opihi, or limpet shells, were used as tools for scooping, scraping, and peeling. Larger cowry shells were used to make scrapers for taro, breadfruit, and grating coconuts. The large cowry was also used as an octopus lure. It was attached to a straight staff with a hook, along with a stone sinker carved in the shape of the cowry. Shells were also used as body adornments for hula dancers. Cowry shells were among the most popular used for lei, bracelets, and anklets. The shells were strung on human hair, woven coconut fibers, or the inner bark (bast) from a variety of trees. On Ni'ihau, the tradition of sewing pūpū 'o Ni'ihau (shells of Ni'ihau) into a lei has been uninterrupted for hundreds of years and has evolved into a fine art that is culturally and economically valuable and protected by law.

In the 1970s came the popular 'opihi shell craze. 'Opihi shells are known as limpet shells. Locals were grinding and polishing the shells to create beautiful necklaces. Since it was a lot of work to grind and polish the 'opihi shells, the shells were used as pendants rather than a complete lei.

In the mid-1970s, the puka shell lei became a must-have craze in Hawai'i and some parts of the U.S. It is still popular today. A puka shell is a cone shell that has been tossed and pounded by the surf. Through erosion, the base of the cone shell is destroyed, leaving only the top disk with a hole in the center. This eroded shell is called the "puka shell," which means "hole" in Hawaiian.

Following the puka shell craze came the paper shell lei craze. A paper shell is a (shell-like) dried disk of a protozoa (one-celled animal), found in the sand at Kailua Beach, O'ahu.

In the early 2000s, the sunrise shell was popular. The sunrise shell is a scallop shell known as Langford's pecten. It is found on the north shores of Kaua'i and O'ahu. Because of its rarity, the shells are used as a pendant rather than a complete lei.

Today, the Hawaiian culture of lei making is alive and thriving. The hobby of shell collecting is a popular pastime for many children and adults in Hawai'i. Modern tools, supplies, methods, procedures, and styles are used, allowing the process of shell lei making to be an enjoyable, satisfying, and relaxing hobby. With a little imagination for combining shells, colors, patterns, stringing, and drilling techniques, the design possibilities are endless.

When collecting shells, collect only the dead shells. Follow the **Sheller's Creed** for ecology-friendly collecting guidance.

Sheller's Creed

The wildlife and natural resources of this world have been entrusted to me for protection and preservation. Whether I wish it or not, I must account to the future for my handling of this wealth today. If I collect shells, I will do it conservatively, recognizing that destruction of the marine habitat, by whatever means, is the true enemy of the sea and its creatures.

Four Rules to Shell By

Leave the live coral heads alone! Look in the rubble, under the slabs, in the sand, and among the loose chunks.

Don't disturb or touch corals.

Be alert for shell eggs and protect them. They have a slim chance of survival, at best. Don't take the mollusk that is guarding them. Avoid disturbing breeding groups.

Collect only what you really need. Take time to examine your finds and leave them to grow and breed if they do not really meet your needs.

Safety Rules

Always use eye protection and a dust mask when grinding, sanding, wire brushing, buffing, or drilling shells. Use a latex paint respirator when spraying a gloss.

Basic Tools

A crafter's workshop should be well-ventilated. It may consist of these few basic tools along with some other simple tools and supplies.

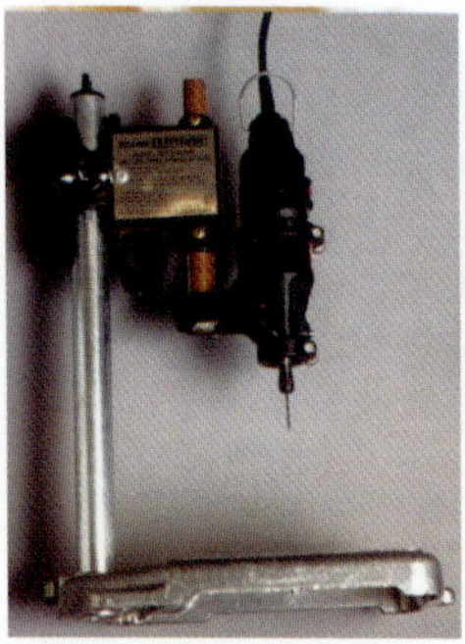

Rotary drill with drill press

Rotary drill with flex shaft and drill press

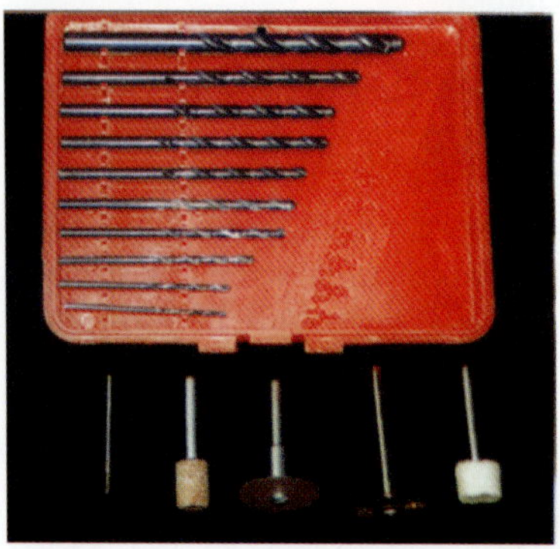

Rotary drill attachments

- Drill bit set
- #60 drill bit
- Sanding cylinder
- Cut-off wheel
- Wire brush
- Polishing wheel

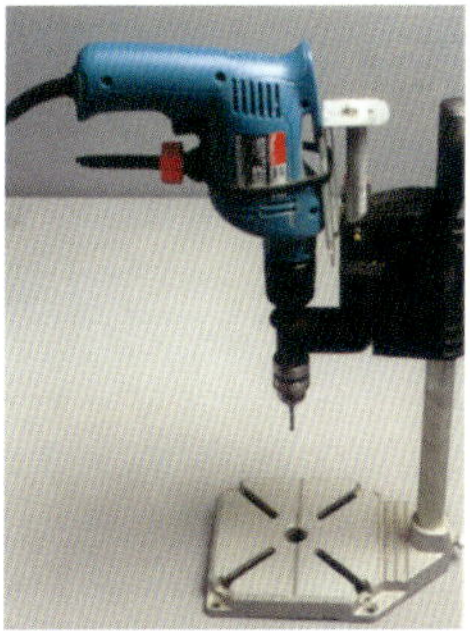

Power drill ½-¾ horse-power and drill press

Power drill 90° position with drill press and sanding flap wheel

Power drill attachments

- Drill bit set
- #60 drill bit
- Sanding flap wheels (medium, and finishing grits)
- Sanding cylinder cone
- Buffing wheel
- Wire brush wheel
- Grinding disk

Basic Procedures

1. Collecting

a. Collect only empty shells.

b. If collecting live shells, use proper shoes (heavy boots with thick rubber soles) and pliable chrome-leather gloves to prevent bites, stings, or pricks from other creatures such as the rockfish *(Synanceja trachynis)* and sea urchins.

c. Beware of cones. Leave live cone shell collecting to the experts. Some species of cones are known to inflict venomous stings causing death. Cones should always be picked up by the wide side of the shell to prevent stinging. If a person is stung, he/she should be immediately taken to the hospital.

d. Follow the **Sheller's Creed** and the **Four Rules to Shell By** on p. 111).

2. Removing mollusks

a. Freeze—Freeze the shells in a watertight bag and cover with water. Freeze at least 24 hours. Thaw shells at room temperature. When completely defrosted, remove the animal tissue using tweezers.

b. Boil—Boil the shells for a few minutes. Remove from the boiling water. Using tweezers or a needle, remove the animal tissue.

c. Bury—Bury the shells in a cardboard box about 18" deep in the soil or sand, or leave out in the yard for at least two months; longer for larger shells. Let the flies, bugs, and ants crawl inside the shells and remove all the animal tissue.

d. Microwave—Microwave the shells for about two minutes; longer for larger shells. Gently, remove the animal tissue using a needle. This is the easiest method for cleaning if you can tolerate the smell in the microwave.

e. Water pick—Squirt high-pressure water into smaller shells pushing out the animal tissue after it has been frozen, boiled, or microwaved.

3. Cleaning

a. Always use eye protection and a dust mask while cleaning shells.

b. Remove sand from aperture using an awl.

c. Rinse thoroughly with fresh water. (Method #1.)

d. Clean the shells with toothpaste, warm water, and a wire brush. Rinse. (Method #2.)

e. Soak in 50:50 bleach and water solution for about 10 minutes. Rub off excess dirt with fingers or a wire brush. Rinse. (Method #3.)

f. Remove the algae and periostracum of shells by soaking them in lukewarm water and 1 tsp. of caustic soda overnight. Brush off the loosened algae and periostracum using a wire brush. Rinse. (Method #4.)

g. Remove the barnacles and other growth using a dental pick or wire brush. Rinse. (Method #5.)

4. Grinding and Sanding

a. Always use eye protection and a dust mask while grinding and sanding shells.
b. Use a drill on a drill press with a grinding disk or flap wheel for thick shells.
c. Use a rotary tool on a drill press stand and a grinding bit for smaller shells.
d. Use a rotary tool drill bit holder for grinding small shells.
e. Anchor the drill press with vice grips when grinding and sanding.
f. Use multi-grit sandpapers to smooth shells.

5. Drilling

a. Use eye protection and a dust mask while drilling shells.
b. Use a vice for safety to hold shells.
c. Use a drill or rotary drill on a drill press stand.
d. Use a rotary drill with a flex shaft for smaller shells.

6. Polishing

a. Use mineral or baby oil.
b. Use a buffing wheel and white rouge compound.
c. Use a polyurethane spray (do not use varnish; it turns yellow).
d. Use a latex paint respirator mask when spraying urethane.

7. Stringing

a. Use a nylon-coated wire.
b. Use a monofilament fishing line.
c. Use a nylon thread.
d. Use a beading string.

8. Maintenance

a. Clean with salt water from the ocean and a toothbrush.
b. Clean with a mix of sea salt and water if you are landlocked.
c. Do not clean with chemicals or place them into chemically treated water.

Basic Lei Making Methods

The following lei are made using these four methods:

Strung Lei Method (Kui)

Straight, single pattern—Kui Pololei

Back-and-forth pattern—Kui Lau or Kui Lu

Knotted or Tied Lei Method

Pīkake style

Sewing with a Needle and Thread

Kui papa, ʻŌlepe

Judd's Pecten Scallop (Fan Shell)

Hawaiian Name: ʻŌlepe

Size: Reaches 27 mm

Found: 20-300 feet deep on sand in colonies and on sandy shores.

Notes: This bivalve, has an upper half that is brown and white and a lower half that is pure white. It is fairly common and endemic to the Hawaiian Islands.

Materials

- Rotary drill
- Rotary drill flex shaft
- Drill bit, 1/16".
- Wooden baseboard
- Pliers, long-nose (as a vice)
- Sewing needle
- Muslin, off-white, thick linen
- Thread, off-white
- Iron

Quantity

- About 300 shells are required for a 25" hat lei sewn with a needle and thread.

Judd's Pecten Scallop shells.

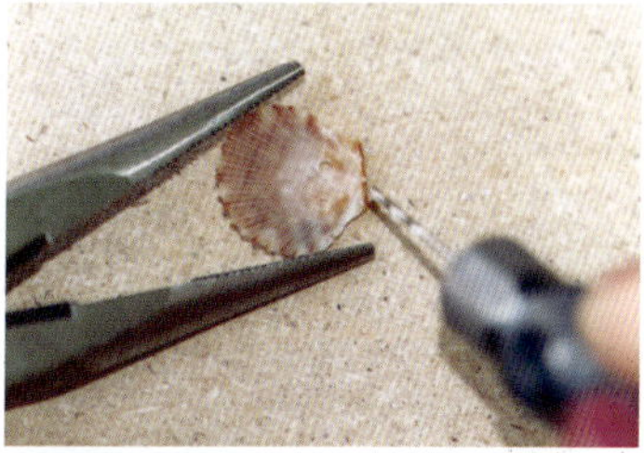

1. Drill two holes at the top of the shell using a rotary drill and flex shaft.

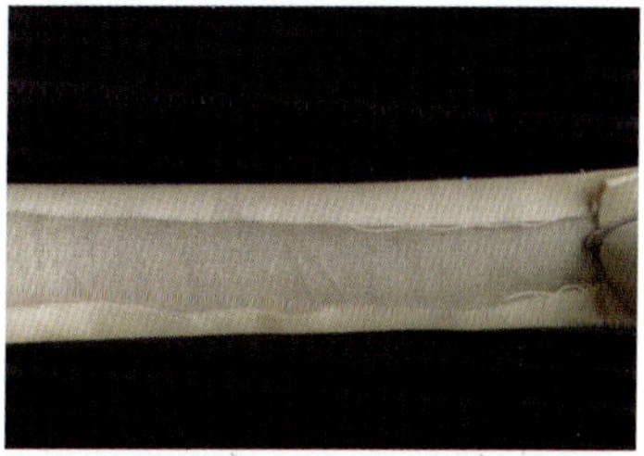

2. Cut a strip of fabric 30" long by 1¾" wide. Fold in the sides of the fabric ¼" on each side. Iron to crease.

3. Thread the needle with double thread knotted at the end. Insert the needle from under the left top fold to hide the mechanics. Stitch on the first shell about ½" from the top of the fabric through the left hole. Pull the thread to the end.

4. Insert the needle down the right hole through the fabric. Pull the thread to the end.

5. Insert the needle up on the outside right of the shell. Pull the thread to the end.

6. Insert the needle back down into the right hole. Pull the thread to the end.

7. Insert the needle up through the left hole. Pull the thread to the end. The thread should be on the outside of the left side of the shell.

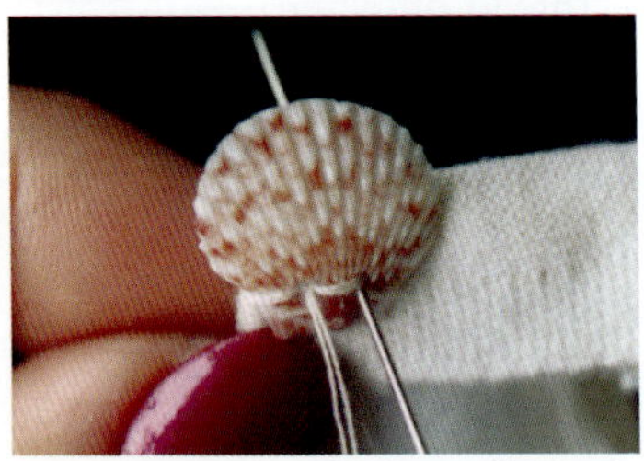

8. Insert the needle down through the right hole. Pull the thread to the end.

9. Add the second shell. Repeat steps #4–9 to secure the second shell.

10. Add the third shell. Repeat steps #4–9 to secure the third shell. Bring the needle back up on the right side of the band then back down on the left side of the band to hide the thread mechanics.

11. Add the second layer of shells about halfway down from the first layer of shells. Repeat steps #4–11 until the desired lei length. To end lei, double fold the end of the fabric above the thread mechanics of the last row of shells. Stitch down to secure. Use a corsage pin to secure the band to a hat.

Judd's Pecten Scallop: Sewn with a needle and thread, hat lei.

Rat Cone

Hawaiian Name: Pūpū ʻalā or Pūpū pōniuniu

Size: Reaches 52 mm

Found: On sandy shores, reef flats, and shallow reefs

Notes: Moderately common in the Hawaiian Islands and the Indo-West Pacific

Rat Cone shells. Tossed, faded shells are purple with a white top, then eventually turn white.

Materials

- Drill
- Drill press stand
- Drill bit, 5/64"
- Wooden baseboard
- Pliers (as a vice)
- Grinding disk
- Buffing wheel
- White rouge polish
- Nylon-coasted wire, .024" diameter
- Closure (see p. 130)

Quantity

- About 35 shells are required for a 30" straight, strung lei.

1. Grind off the tip of the shell using a grinding disk.

2. Drill a hole from the top of the shell stopping at the aperture. Do not drill through the base of the shell. Hold the shell with a vice for safety.

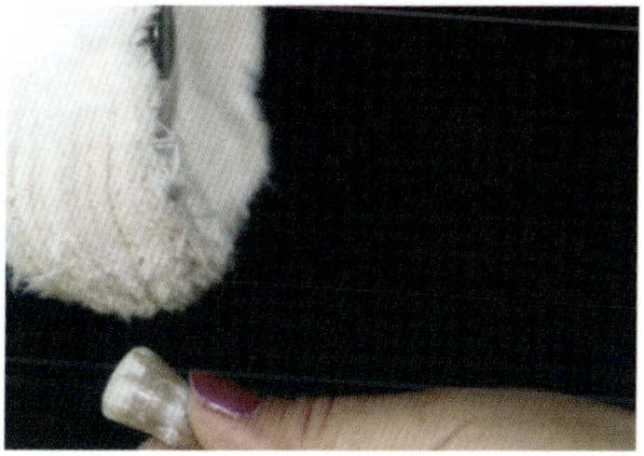

3. Polish the shell using a buffing wheel and white rouge polish.

4. Arrange the shells into stringing order, larger shells in the center. String half of the shells onto a wire from the top of the shell through the aperture, smallest to largest. Cut the wire long enough to complete the lei. String the other half of the shells onto the wire from the top of the shell through the aperture. Start with the largest shell first creating the downward look. Continue until the smallest shell. See p. 130 for closure method.

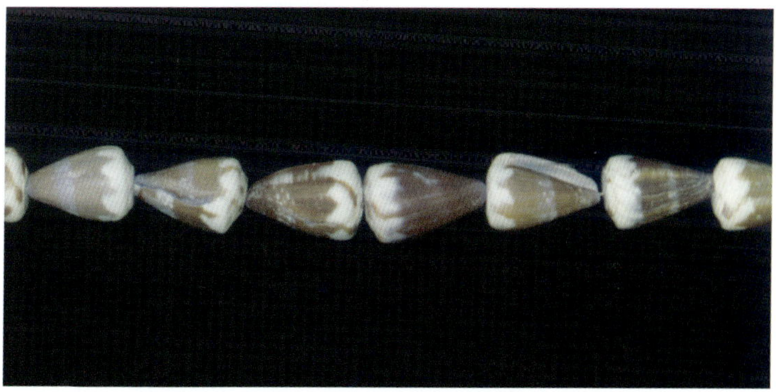

Rat Cone: Straight, strung lei.

Variable Dove

Hawaiian Name: Momi or Hālili

Size: Reaches 10 mm

Found: In shallow water to 4 feet, under rocks in tide pools and on sandy shores.

Notes: Abundant in the Hawaiian Islands and the Indo-West Pacific. Popular in the Ni'ihau shell lei. Momi shells come in a variety of eight colors and patterns. Each has a descriptive Hawaiian name based on its colors and patterns.

Materials

- Nail clippers
- Awl
- Nylon thread
- Quick-drying cement or bee's wax
- Closure (see p. 130)

Quantity

- About 360 shells are required for a 30" pīkake style, knotted lei. Allow about 30-50 percent additional shells for damage while piercing.

Variable Dove (Momi) shells come in a variety of colors ranging from white, tan, bluish-brown, brown, black, and red-spotted.

1. Clip off the tip of the shell using a nail clipper.

2. Pierce the shell near the aperture, in the middle of the shell, using an awl.

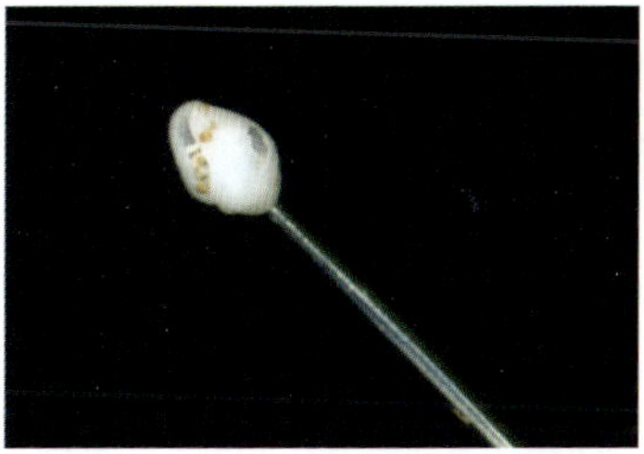

3. Puncture the shell from the tip down to the drilled hole using an awl.

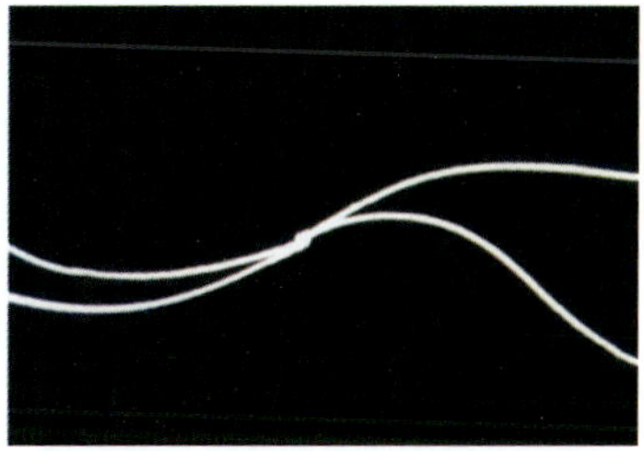

4. Cut two pieces of thread to the length of the desired lei, plus 10" to allow for the knots and closure. Tie a knot dividing the two threads into halves. Insert the ends of the thread into the tube of quick-drying cement or bee's wax to create a stiff point.

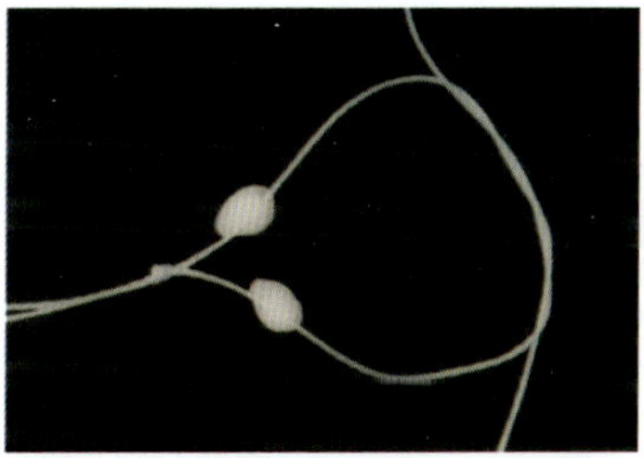

5. Arrange the shells into stringing order, larger shells in the center. String the first half of the shells onto the first set of two threads. String one shell on each thread from the pierced hole through the tip of the shell.

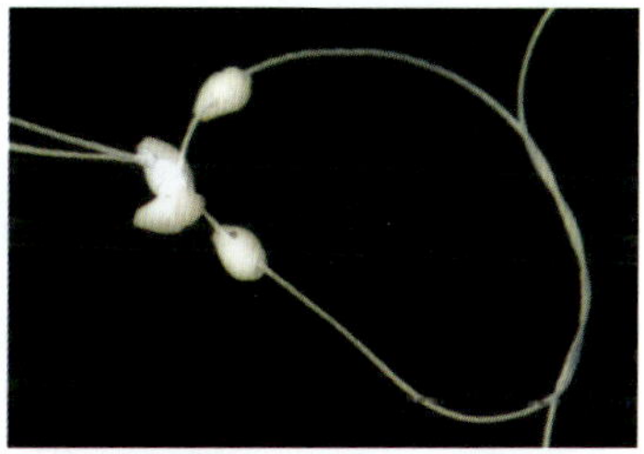

6. Tie a single knot to secure the two shells in place. Keep the shell pattern consistent and balanced. Don't twist the threads while tying. Repeat steps #6 and #7 until the first half of the shells are strung.

7. String the second half of shells onto the second set of the threads. Insert the thread from the drilled hole of the shell out through the aperture. This procedure allows the center two shells to be faced bottom-to-bottom with each other. Continue until the second half of the shells are strung. See p. 130 for closure methods.

Variable Dove: Pīkake style, knotted lei.

Furrowed Limpet

Hawaiian Name: 'Opihi makaiauli

Size: Reaches 55 mm

Found: In shallow water; splash zones on rocky coast.

Notes: 'Opihi gathering is very dangerous due to strong waves. Leave to experts. Edible. As of this printing, Hawai'i state fishing regulations allow collection of limpets with a shell diameter greater than 1¼". Endemic to the Hawaiian Islands.

Materials

- Drill
- Drill press stand
- Grinding disk
- Sanding flap wheels, #120 and a finishing grit
- Buffing wheel
- Buffing polish, white Tripoli and white rouge
- Drill bit, 3/32"
- Sandpaper, #120 and #320
- Quick-drying clear cement or clear-drying glue
- Rubber bands
- Satin ribbon, #3
- Ribbon Needle

Quantity

- About 36 shells are required for a 30″ straight, strung lei.

Furrowed Limpet shells.

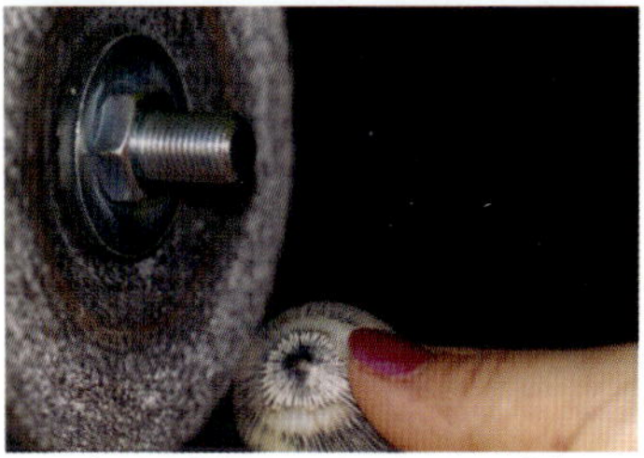

1. Grind off the outer layer of the shell until reaching the whitish color.

2. Sand smooth with a 120-grit flap wheel, followed by a finishing flap wheel.

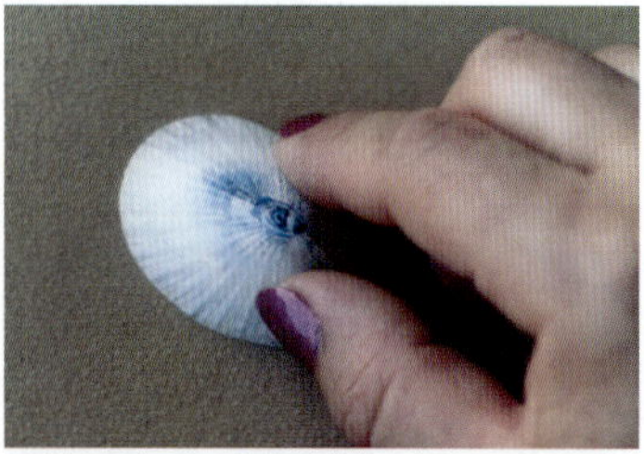

3. Hand sand the base to even the surface.

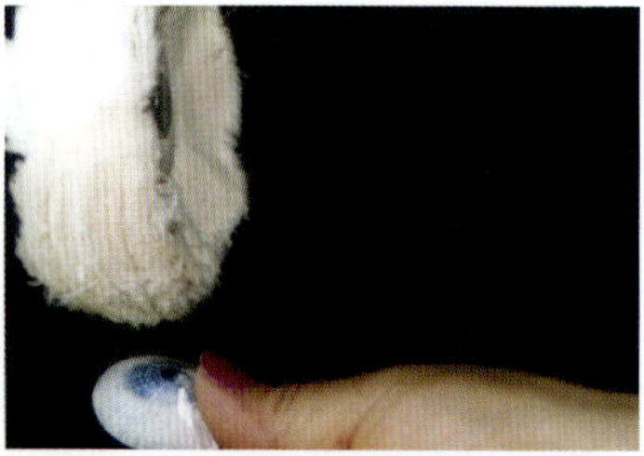

4. Buff with white rouge. If scratches are shown on the shell, continue to hand sand and buff until smooth.

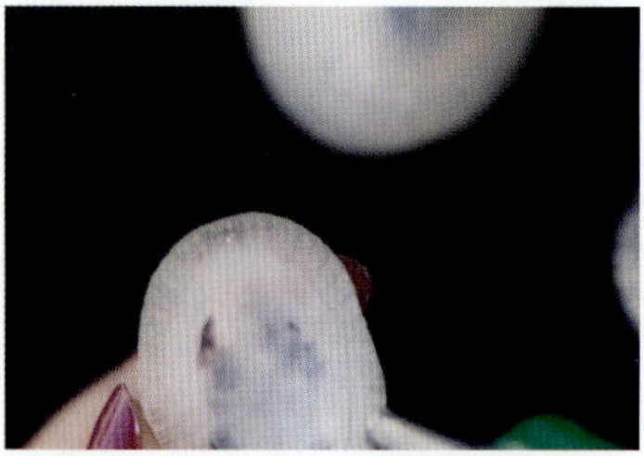

5. Group the shells into sets of two having identical sizes. Glue the sets together from the inside of the shell, using a clear-drying cement.

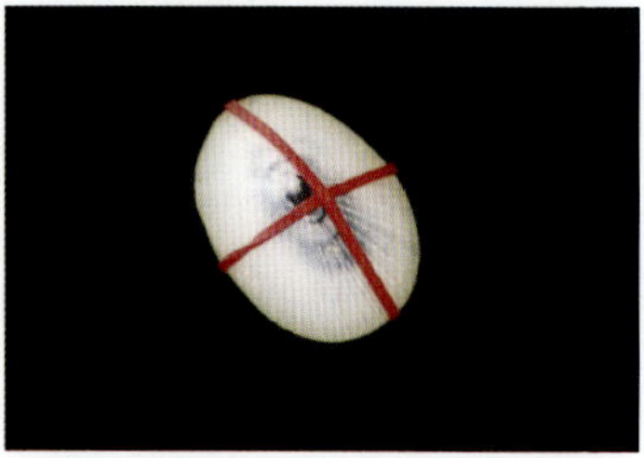

6. Bind the glued shells together with rubber bands. Let the glue dry for 24 hours. If the shells are uneven or scratched, hand sand to smooth the shell and buff to shine.

7. Drill a hole through the top and bottom of the shell using a 3/32". drill bit on a drill press. Hand sand to smooth the drilled edges.

8. Arrange the shells into stringing order, larger shells in the center. Cut a piece of ribbon to the length of the shells, plus 30" to allow for the knots and closure. Tie a knot about 10" from the end of the ribbon. String the first shell onto the ribbon using a Ribbon Needle™. Pull the shell down to the end of the ribbon.

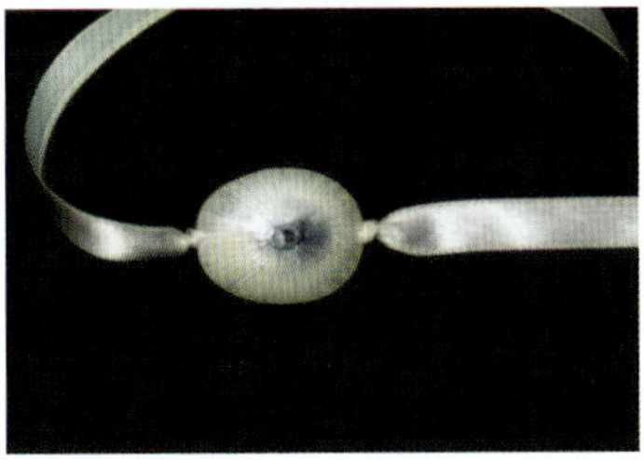

9. Tie a single knot after each shell to secure it in place. Continue until half of the shells are strung and knotted.

10. Reverse the direction of the shells for the second half of the lei so the shells face in an upward pattern. Repeat steps #9 and #10 to complete the lei. Trim the remaining ribbon leaving 10" to tie. Tie a bow to close the lei.

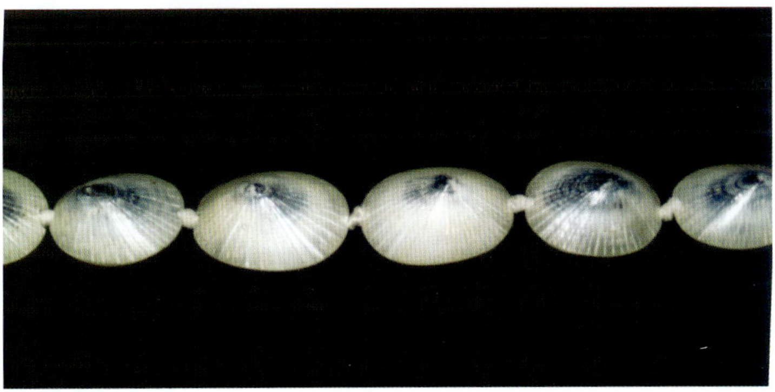

Furrowed Limpet: Straight, strung lei.

Nerite Pipipi

Hawaiian Name: Pipipi
Size: Reaches 15 mm
Found: Splash zones on rock just above the waterline.
Notes: Abundant in the Hawaiian Islands and various localities in the Pacific. Edible.

Nerite Pipipi shells.

Materials

- Rotary drill
- Rotary drill press
- Drill bit, #60
- Wooden baseboard
- Pliers, longnose (as a vice)
- Mineral or baby oil
- Nylon-coated wire, .015" diameter, or monofilament fishing line 12-lb. test
- Tweezers, longnose
- Closure (see p. 130)

Quantity

- About 110 shells are required for a 30" back-and-forth patterned lei.

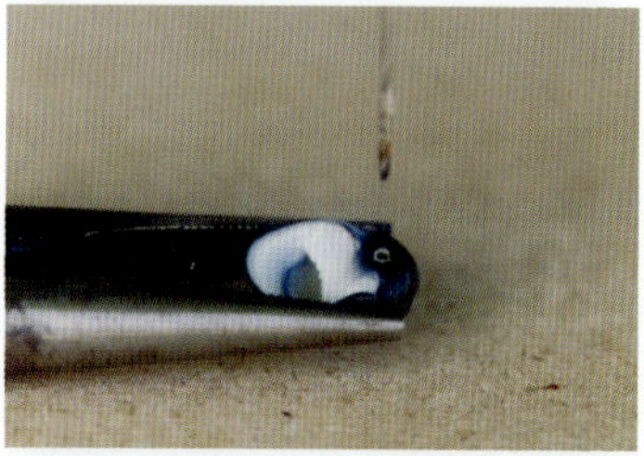

1. Drill a hole in the center of the tip using a #60 drill bit. Hold the shell with a vice for safety.

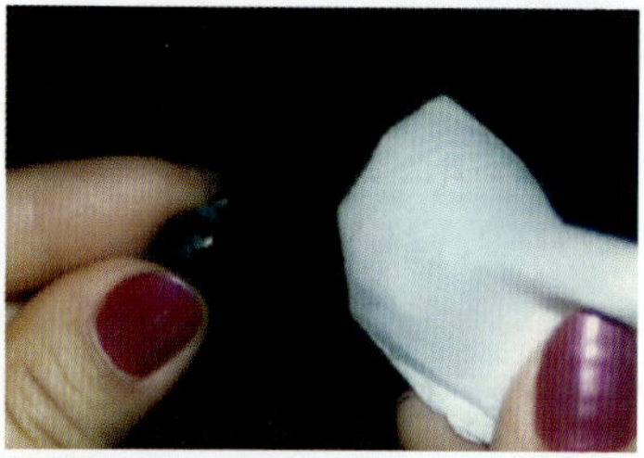

2. Shine the shell with mineral oil. Wipe off the excess oil.

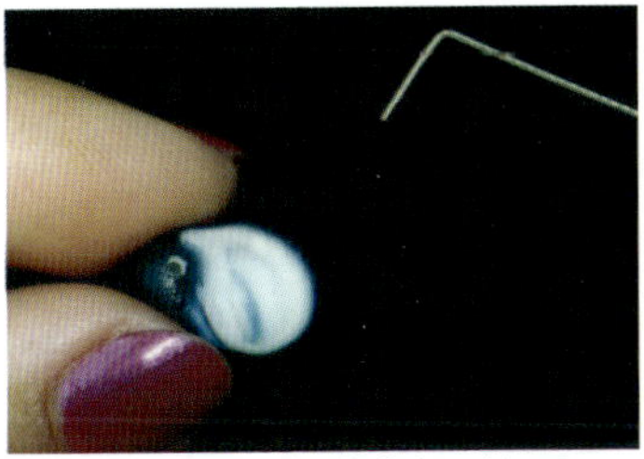

3. Arrange the shells into stringing order, larger shells in the center. Bend the wire into a 90° angle. String the shells onto the wire from the drilled hole through the aperture.

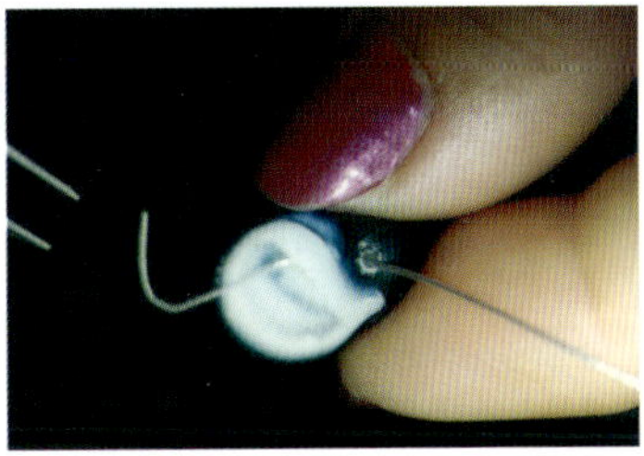

4. Grab the tip of the wire with tweezers if needed.

5. Position the shells in a back-and-forth pattern. Repeat until desired length. See p. 130 for closure method.

Nerite Pipipi: Back-and-forth, strung lei.

Clasp Closure

Materials

- 1 Lobster claw clasp (or similar)
- 1 Toggle clasp, loop (or similar)
- 2 Bead crimps (or similar)
- 2 Puka shells
- 1 Crimping pliers
- 1 Wire cutters, diagonal

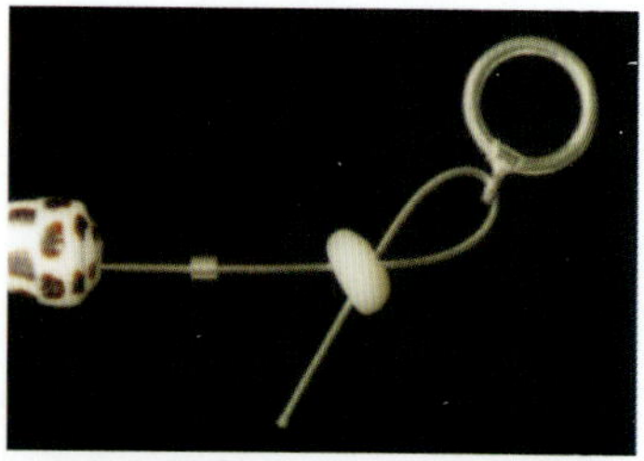

1. String the first wire through a crimp, a puka shell, a toggle loop, then back into the puka shell.

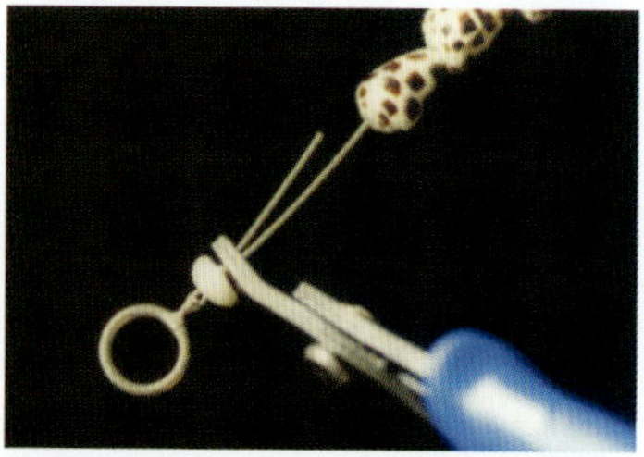

2. Insert the end of the wire back into the crimp bead. Tighten the wire. Flatten the crimp using crimping pliers. Trim off the excess wire using a diagonal wire cutter.

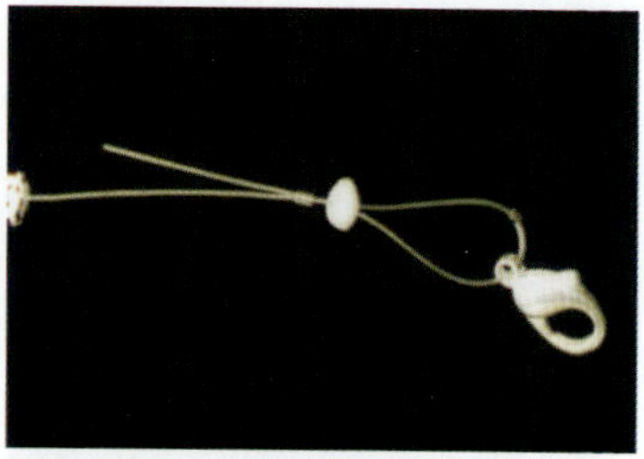

3. Pull the shells down toward the loop closure. Insert the second wire through a crimp, puka shell, lobster claw, and back into the crimp. Repeat step #2 to complete the closure.

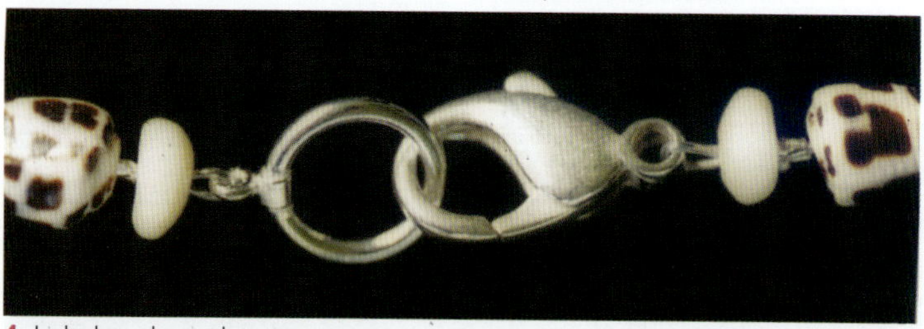

4. Lobster claw closure.

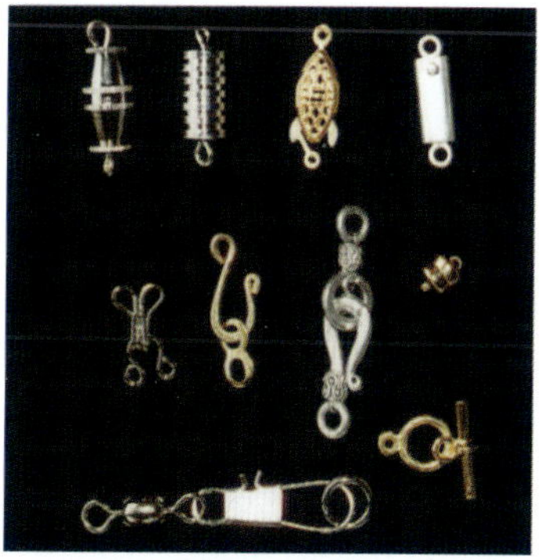

5. Samples of clasps: barrel, box, hook-and-eye, magnet, toggle, and interlock snap swivel.

Hawai'i's School Colors

O'ahu High Schools & Colleges/Universities

'Aiea High School	green, white
American Renaissance Academy	red, black, white, gold
Āneuenue School	teal, blue
Asia Pacific International School Hawai'i	green, red
Assets High School	blue, white, red
Calvary Chapel Christian School	maroon, gold, navy blue
Campbell High School	black, orange
Castle High School	maroon, gold
Christian Academy	royal blue, white
Damien Memorial School	purple, gold
Farrington High School	maroon, white
Friendship Christian Schools	green, silver
Hakipu'u Academy	black, gold
Halau Ku Mana PCS	red, gold, green
Hanalani Schools	royal purple, gold
Hawai'i Baptist Academy	gold, black, white
Hawai'i School for the Deaf and Blind	emerald green, white
Hawai'i Technology Academy	green, black, white
Hawaiian Mission Academy	blue, white
'Iolani School	black, red, white
Island Pacific Academy	navy blue, gold, silver
Kahuku High School	red, white
Kailua High School	blue, white
Kaimukī Christian School	royal blue, white
Kaimukī High School	green, gold
Kaiser High School	blue, gold
Kalāheo High School	blue, orange
Kalani High School	red, white
Kamaile Academy PCS	silver, blue
Kamehameha Schools-Kapalama	blue, white
Kapolei High School	teal, silver

Ke Kula 'O Samuel M. Kamakau LPCS .... blue, brown
Ko'olau Baptist Academy .... royal blue, white
La Pietra Hawai'i School for Girls .... royal blue, powder blue
Lanakila Baptist School .... red, white
Le Jardin Academy .... blue, white
Leilehua High School .... green gold
Maili Bible Church & School .... baby blue, black
Maryknoll School .... maroon, gold
McKinley High School .... black, gold
Mid-Pacific Institute .... green, white
Mililani High School .... brown, gold
Moanalua High School .... royal blue, silver
Myron Thompson Academy NCPCS .... black, silver
Nānākuli High School .... black, gold
Olomana School .... green
Pacific Buddhist Academy .... gold, teal, indigo
Pearl City High School .... purple, white
Punahou School .... buff, blue
Radford High School .... black, red, white
Roosevelt High School .... red, gold
Sacred Hearts Academy .... white, gold
St. Andrew's Schools-The Priory .... red, white
St. Louis School .... blue, red
St. Michael School .... navy blue, gold
Trinity Christian School .... blue, white
University Laboratory School .... green, white
Wai'anae High School .... red, blue
Waialua High School .... scarlet, gray
Waipahu High School .... navy blue, gold
Brigham Young University Hawai'i (winter) ...... crimson, gold
Chaminade University .... white, blue, silver
Hawai'i Pacific University .... teal, blue-gray
Hawai'i Tokai International College .... white, dark blue
UH Honolulu Community College .... teal
UH Kap'iolani Community College .... blue
UH Leeward Community College .... blue
UH Windward Community College .... green

University of Hawai'i at Manoa .... green
University of Hawai'i–West O'ahu .... red

Big Island High Schools

Christian Liberty Academy .... navy blue, orange
Connections PCS black, white, forest green, silver
Hawai'i Academy of Arts & Sciences PCS .... silver, blue
Hawai'i Preparatory Academy .... red, white
Hilo High School .... blue, gold
Honoka'a High School .... green, gold
Kamehameha School–Hawai'i .... blue, white
Kanu o ka 'Āina NCPCS .... red, yellow
Ka'ū High School .... maroon, white
Ke Ana La'ahana PCS .... no set colors
Ke Kula 'O Nāwahīokalani'ōpu Iki Lab PCS .... red, yellow, black
Ke Kula 'O 'Ehunuikaimalino .... red, yellow
Kea'au High School .... navy blue, red
Kealakehe High School .... blue, silver
Kohala High School .... black, gold
Konawaena High School .... green, white
Laupahoehoe Community PCS .... royal blue, gold
Makua Lani Christian Academy .... purple, white
Pahoa High School .... green, white
Parker School .... black, maroon, white
St. Joseph School .... red, gold
Waiakea High School .... navy blue, white
West Hawai'i Explorations Academy .... teal, silver

Big Island Colleges and Universities

UH Hawai'i Community College–Hilo .... maroon
UH Hawai'i Community College–Palamanui .... maroon
University of Hawai'i–Hilo .... red

Kaua'i Schools and College

Island School .... blue, gold
Kanuikapono PCS .... navy, sky blue, smoke gray
Kapa'a High School .... green, white
Kaua'i Christian Academy .... teal, white
Kaua'i High School .... red, white
Kawaikini NCPCS .... teal, brown
Ke Kula Ni'ihau O Kekaha Learning Center .... gold ,white
Kula Aupuni Ni'ihau A Kahelelani Aloha NCPCS .... purple, white
Ni'ihau High School .... no set colors
Olelo Christian Academy .... teal, gray, black
Waimea High School .... blue, white
UH Kaua'i Community College .... purple

Maui Schools and Colleges

Doris Todd Christian Academy .... blue, green
H.P. Baldwin High School .... maroon, columbia blue
Haleakala Waldorf School–Kulanui Campus .... teal, yellow
Hāna High School .... green, gold
Ka'ahumanu Hou Christian School .... purple, silver
Kamehameha Schools–Maui .... blue, white
Kihei Charter School .... blue, silver, black
King Kekaulike High School .... black, teal

Lahainaluna High School..red, white
Maui High School..royal blue, white
Maui Preparatory Academy..green, navy blue
Seabury Hall School..red, blue
St. Anthony School..navy blue, gold
University of Hawai'i Maui College..blue

Lāna'i & Moloka'i Schools

Lāna'i High School..green, gold
Moloka'i High School..green, white, black

This book is an abridgment and combination of the following books published by Mutual Publishing:

Crochet Lei-Making in Hawai'i: A Step-by-Step Guide by Judy Dela Cruz, published in2005

Crochet Lei-Making in Hawai'i, Volume 2: A Step-by-Step Guide by Judy Dela Cruz, published in 2006

Crochet Lei-Making in Hawai'i, Volume 3: A Step-by-Step Guide to Crochet, Straw and Rickrack Sewn Leis by Judy Dela Cruz, published in 2009

Hawaiian Lei Making: A Step-by-Step Guide by Laurie Shimizu Ide, published in 1998

Hawaiian Shell Lei Making: A Step-by-Step Guide by Laurie Shimizu Ide, published in 2005

Money Lei Making in Hawai'i 2: A Step-by-Step Guide by Laurie Shimizu Ide, published in 2008